DIANE SAWYER

Super Newswoman

Rose Blue and Joanne E. Bernstein

—Contemporary Women Series—

ENSLOW PUBLISHERS, INC.

Bloy St. & Ramsey Ave.   P.O. Box 38
Box 777   Aldershot
Hillside, NJ 07205   Hants GU12 6BP
U.S.A.   U.K.

Library of Congress Cataloging-in-Publication Data:

Blue, Rose.
   Diane Sawyer: super newswoman / by Rose Blue and Joanne E. Bernstein.
      p. cm. (Contemporary women series)
   Includes index
   Summary: A biography of the television journalist who joined the staff of "60
Minutes" as that show's first female correspondent.
   ISBN 0-89490-288-1
   1. Sawyer, Diane, 1945-   —Juvenile literature. 2. Television
journalists—United States—Biography—Juvenile literature.
3. Television personalities—United States—Biography—Juvenile
literature. [1. Sawyer, Diane, 1945-   . 2. Television
journalists. 3. Television personalities.] I. Bernstein, Joanne
E. II. Title. III. Series.
PN4874.S298B57 1990
070'.92—dc20   89-16817
[B]   CIP
[92]   AC

Printed in the United States of America

10 9 8 7 6 5 4 3 2 1

Illustration Credits:
AP/Wide World Photos, pp. 94, 98; Courtesy of CBS News, *60 MINUTES*, pp. 4, 9, 73, 83;
Copyright © 1981, *The Courier Journal*. Reprinted with permission from *The Courier-Jour-
nal*, pp. 22, 35, 61; Albert Einstein College of Medicine, pp. 67, 78; Louisville Convention
and Visitors Bureau, pp. 12, 15; U.S. National Archives, Nixon Presidential Materials Staff,
pp. 39, 45, 47, 50, 54; Wellesley College Archives, pp. 18, 28, 33.

Cover Illustration: Courtesy of CBS News, *60 MINUTES*

Contents

A CBS glamour "publicity" shot of Diane Sawyer.

Introduction

From its beginnings in the late 1960s, CBS television's *60 Minutes* had been one of America's most watched news programs. In many homes across the United States, Sunday night is not complete without *60 Minutes*. Each program usually covers three different stories, plus some witty commentary and perhaps a look at mail from viewers. Each story is presented by one of the program's reporters, who are known as correspondents. They may point out corruption in government or tell of the evil deeds of countries or corporations. The stories often discuss bad or sad things that have happened to individuals, and why. Sometimes, though, the features are more lighthearted and uplifting—a profile of comedian Steve Martin, for example.

Even though the show is very popular, it is sometimes criticized for giving only one side of the story. Critics say it paints a picture that is too dark or too bleak. Or that it is more interested in show business than in news. Whether the criticisms are well founded or not, the stories that *60 Minutes* tells usually make the American public sit up and take notice.

Throughout its very successful first sixteen years, *60 Minutes* was hard-hitting and challenging. It was also all male.

Today, *60 Minutes* is still hard-hitting and challenging. But in 1984, its "all-male" image changed when thirty-eight-year-old Diane Sawyer joined the staff as its first female correspondent. This diligent, experienced, and attractive journalist became part of television's "million-dollar men's club."

To be a correspondent on *60 Minutes* means to be in the highest rank of TV broadcasters. It also means to be in a constant fight for news stories. Unlike most other shows—and most other businesses, in fact—there are no meetings at *60 Minutes*. Diane Sawyer didn't meet with the show's other correspondents to discuss "who does what" on forthcoming programs. Unlike other shows and other businesses (and *60 Minutes* is *big* business), there are few rules. Each story idea that is approved has a correspondent and one or more producers, who act as editors and reporters.

How do the stories get approved? Either correspondents or producers can suggest story ideas. Whoever can persuade the executive producer, Don Hewitt, of the merit of an idea gets to work on that story. The stories that the audience enjoys are the result of one correspondent or producer reaching Hewitt first to say, "Have you thought about such-and-such?" or "What do you think of profiling so-and-so?" Sawyer has called it a "full-scale war." War or not, it keeps the correspondents on their toes. The pursuit of the interesting story is so hot that a producer or correspondent who has a winning idea for Don Hewitt has been known to follow him into the men's room to sell it. With Diane there, the joke around *60 Minutes* was that even though the show had reached a kind of equality with women producers and one woman correspondent, the "bathroom chase" kept women just slightly unequal!

Until Diane Sawyer left the CBS network for ABC in early 1989, she was one of six correspondents on *60 Minutes*. The others are familiar faces to most television watchers. They are Mike

Wallace, Ed Bradley, Harry Reasoner, and Morley Safer; and in addition, Andy Rooney does commentary on odd, funny aspects of life. What did these long-time newsmen and television personalities think of having this newcomer in their midst?

Mike Wallace might be called the dean of the *60 Minutes* correspondents. He has been slugging out tough news stories for more than thirty years. Like the other correspondents, he soon took Diane pretty much for granted on the show. He remembers their first meeting when they were both working in Washington, D.C. There were no walls between their small cubbyhole offices, and Wallace says that he could always hear her talking on the telephone. Diane's voice was soft, he recalls, but she was very persistent. He remembers thinking that she was a reporter "who worked very, very hard." He still thinks so.

Everyone develops his or her own style on *60 Minutes*. Diane Sawyer would develop hers, Mike Wallace said when she first went on the show. He also thought early on that she might become a "major figure in broadcast journalism," a prediction that has indeed come to pass.

Ed Bradley remembered Diane from back in the late 1970s. They were both "outcasts at the White House" in 1978, said Bradley. The heads of the CBS Washington bureau didn't care very much for Sawyer because she was too close to President Richard Nixon and his administration. (In 1974 Nixon became the first U.S. president ever to resign, as a result of a government scandal called the Watergate affair.) The CBS chiefs didn't like Sawyer, and they didn't pay much attention to Bradley. He had never worked for CBS News before, so he was "low man on the totem pole."

Bradley admires Sawyer just for surviving her hectic first year on *60 Minutes*. After joining the show himself in 1981, Bradley had seven months (from February to September) to prepare before he had to go on the air with his first story. Diane's case was different, he says. She just had to "jump right into the frying pan." Her first story was about Velma Barfield, a grandmother who was on Death Row for murder. Barfield was about to be executed when Diane joined *60 Minutes,* so the story had to go on the air almost immediately. That was Diane's introduction to her new job. The pace never let up.

Harry Reasoner regarded Diane Sawyer as a good *60 Minutes* reporter. What did he mean by that? "She is willing to let her ego and her comfort take second place to the story," Reasoner says. "You have to do that to be good in this business." He also thought she fit in well with the rest of the show's crew.

Morley Safer said that Diane had something else that is very important. It's something that the rest of them brought to the show as well—"good reporting instincts." He also stated that in general it's harder for a woman to be on *60 Minutes* than it is for a man. That's because, says Safer, right or wrong, women "get looked at more than men do" when they're on television. However, Diane knows how to get people to look past her physical appearance and presentation and concentrate on the story.

Andy Rooney finds it hard to say anything without being funny. He commented that he sometimes wished Diane were homely because "she's such a good reporter" that "it's almost a shame she's burdened with such good looks."

Don Hewitt, the producer of *60 Minutes,* was directly responsible for hiring Diane. As soon as she joined the program, he was asked why he hadn't hired a woman before. His answer? "Because there wasn't a Diane Sawyer before." For Hewitt, "a good reporter is a good reporter is a good reporter." Hewitt has said he was not looking for a woman in particular. Instead, when he hires a correspondent, he's searching for the best broadcaster available. Hewitt says that besides getting to the meat of a story, Sawyer makes the television screen light up with her presence. She knows just when to pause, just where to put stress on a word. Not all television reporters can do that, and do it well. Diane knows how.

What did Diane Sawyer think of Diane Sawyer on *60 Minutes*? Soon after she joined the show, she told an interviewer that her secret desire was to be a "backup singer to Bette Midler." But she must have said it with a big smile. Anyone who knows Diane or has worked with her probably thinks that her years with *60 Minutes* were spent doing what she wanted to do. She reported thoroughly, intelligently, and honestly on the stories that kept the American public sitting in front of television sets every Sunday night.

But despite her love for the work and her important position on

Diane spends most of her busy day at her desk, not in front of the camera.

60 Minutes, and despite CBS's frantic efforts to keep her, early in 1989 the ABC network announced that it had signed a contract with Sawyer. "I'm grateful for every moment at CBS," newspapers quoted Diane as saying.

Then why did she leave? Probably because CBS, even though paying her an annual salary of more than $1 million, could not, or did not, offer her the job she has really always wanted. Diane Sawyer joined ABC to become coanchor, with former White House correspondent San Donaldson, on a new program called *Prime Time Live*. Even back in Kentucky, Diane was always heading for an anchor spot.

1

Back Home in Kentucky

How do you get to the very top in television journalism? The same way you get to the very top in anything else. You must study hard and have an immense capacity for work.

For Diane Sawyer, the studying began "back home" in Kentucky. She was born a pre-Christmas baby (given name Lila Diane) on December 22, 1945. Her hometown is Glasgow, in the southern part of the commonwealth. (Kentucky is one of four U.S. states that are called commonwealths; the name means "common well-being." The other three are Massachusetts, Pennsylvania, and Virginia.)

Kentucky's nickname is the Bluegrass State, for the greenish-blue tinge of the grasses that grow abundantly there. It is an agricultural region, but it is also known for coal mining and horse racing. Each spring Kentucky makes national and international headlines with its running of the classic Kentucky Derby. This horse race for three-year-olds takes place at the famous Churchill Downs, the one-and-a-quarter-mile course in Louisville.

Glasgow, a small farm town of a few thousand, is the seat of Barren County. Diane's father was E. P. Sawyer, known as Tom. He was trained as a lawyer and became a county administrative judge. His other interests included composing country music. Diane's mother, Jean, taught elementary school. Diane was the second of two girls born to the Sawyers. Her sister Linda had entered the family three years earlier.

Not long after Diane's birth, the Sawyer foursome moved north from their small community to Louisville, home of the Kentucky Derby and the state's largest city. The plans for the city of Louisville were laid out back in 1779, ten years before the United States

Diane Sawyer grew up in Louisville, Kentucky, home of America's most famous horse race, the Kentucky Derby. Shown here is the racetrack, Churchill Downs, where each May the Derby is held.

became a country. It did not officially become a city until 1828. Louisville sits on the banks of the Ohio River, a border it shares with Indiana. It boasts the oldest city university in the United States—the University of Louisville, founded in 1798.

Although Diane did not stay on in Louisville to attend the university (except for some law courses in later years), Louisville was where she spent her elementary and high school years.

Diane's natural talents and abilities are stressed consistently by those who knew her in the early years. Her Aunt Lila Farmer says, "Diane was always alert. She was sweet, clever, and funny." Aunt Lila recalls taking her niece, then a preschooler, to a performance of *Peter Pan*. "She was so thrilled. She had an amazing understanding of the play for her age." Says Mrs. Farmer proudly, "I would have bet on her even then."

There is probably not a child on earth who would want to have his or her mother (or father) for a schoolteacher! But that's exactly what happened to Diane in the third grade in her Louisville school. Mrs. Sawyer was Diane's teacher that year. Diane can still remember some of her scoldings. She especially remembers that her mother tried to teach her a lesson in being prepared by calling on her in class one day, knowing that she didn't know the Roman numeral for nine. (It's IX.) Diane was embarrassed, but she didn't forget the lesson in doing one's work. Her organized routine for work today reflects that continual striving to be prepared.

Diane denies that her parents pushed her into doing well. But they and her older sister certainly set vivid examples for her to follow. Her sister Linda was very talented. Attractive and smart, as Diane was, Diane was always somewhat in Linda's shadow. Or at least Diane thought so.

Perhaps that is why, during her school years, Diane was happy to take part in the family's desire for their children to be, in her words, "madly extracurricular." Diane wanted to take "every imaginable lesson on earth."

Besides her regular school classes, over the years Diane took lessons in fencing, horseback riding, ballet, tap dance, piano, and voice. She also studied the classical guitar and took part in children's theater. Her mother urged her to take all those lessons, says Diane. But her mother wasn't pushing her in any particular direction, she adds. It was just that Jean Sawyer had never had the chance to do any of those things herself. She wanted to make sure her children had the opportunities she had missed. And perhaps, in Diane's eyes, all those extra skills would let her shine, as her sister Linda did.

Both of Diane's parents had grown up deep in the heart of Kentucky. Both had been born of English and Irish ancestors. Diane's grandfathers had the wonderful-sounding names of Pappy Jim and Foxy Dunagan (her mother's father). Foxy was a tough farmer who began work at the age of eight to support a younger brother and sister when his father died. He couldn't even reach the handles of the family plow. But that wasn't going to stop him from farming. He built an extension on the handles and plowed the fields.

Diane's mother had inherited a good deal of the strength and tough-mindedness of Foxy Dunagan. In contrast, Diane's father was more spiritual. He was both intellectual and religious. He founded the local Methodist church, and both his daughters sang in the choir. Diane also played the organ there.

Diane and her family were very much the image of middle America. She once joked about a particular family portrait, taken when she was seventeen. Everyone looked handsome and blond, or as Diane said, as if they all belonged on a box of corn flakes.

Diane was a good student at Seneca High School in Louisville and did well in all her other extra lessons, too. She also found time to be a cheerleader and basketball player and joined every additional club she could. Perhaps as an omen of the future, she became the editor in chief of the school newspaper, called the *Arrow*.

Mrs. Mildred Kraft Cox was a teacher at Seneca High back then.

She served as faculty adviser of the *Arrow* when Diane was its editor in chief. Says Mrs. Cox, "Diane was one of the nicest and most competent students I ever knew." She was exceptionally versed in writing and language arts. As now, Diane was outstanding and beautiful.

Mrs. Cox describes Diane as a "take-charge girl in the nicest possible way." She says that Diane not only got things done but did so without bruising anyone's feelings. Diane was popular, and her

The skyline of Louisville, the state's largest city. It was settled in 1778 and named for King Louis XVI of France.

fellow students did not seem to resent her popularity or the publicity that was to surround her even in high school. After Diane won the state title in a beauty contest, that sent her on to compete for (and win) the title of "Junior Miss," the staff of the Seneca yearbook unveiled a huge poster with the affectionate words "Our Junior Miss" written on it in bold letters. They also presented her with a large box of candy. Diane has quipped about the gift, "I guess they wanted me plump for the Mobile contest" (where the final Junior Miss contest was held). This kind of uncertainty about her powers has always been a thread in Diane Sawyer's life—at home, in school, even today in the workplace.

Kenneth B. Farmer, the principal of Seneca High School, now retired, and brother-in-law to Lila Farmer, tells the same story as countless others. All the stories are more confident than Diane's. He says, "Diane was an honor student from seventh grade on. It would be easier to list the things she didn't accomplish. That list would be far smaller."

Others on the *Arrow* describe their editor as a good sport, friendly, with a sense of humor. She was a girl who balanced her studies and extracurricular activities with occasional parties and dances. A girl who made her time count.

The "Seneca Salute" column of the high school yearbook reads:

> Throughout the commonwealth Diane is known as Miss Junior Miss of Kentucky. We are proud of her for this achievement, but Diane possesses far more than beauty and talent. She is a good student, a wonderful friend, and a reliable supporter of all school activities, both educational and extracurricular. Yes after dedicating two former years to the *Arrow*, she is Editor-in-Chief of the book you are reading right now. Diane, your modesty and humility are an integral part of your charm. Your fine example of good leadership deserves the highest praise.

Diane was also a member of the National Honor Society. Membership in the society was the highest honor a student could receive because selections were made by a group of faculty members on the basis of character, scholarship, leadership, and service.

Young Diane Sawyer could definitely be called an overachiever. Surprisingly enough, she says she was "insecure and boringly serious." Despite all her activities in school and out, she felt like a shy person. "Part of me longed to be like the other girls, to wisecrack, flirt, and ride in open cars, screaming with pleasure," she told an interviewer. "But part of me wanted nothing to do with it, and I was something of a loner instead." When Diane was not invited to her senior prom, she says she didn't care, or cry. But her English teacher *was* provoked to tears at the thought that this teacher's favorite had been overlooked. Diane went to a movie on prom night and had her own kind of special evening.

Diane preferred to spend whatever spare time there was with a couple of girlfriends and her close male friend, Greg Haynes. Nearly every day this small group would go off to a nearby creek to sit and talk among the trees, or as they called it, to "commune with nature." They called themselves "reincarnated transcendentalists," meaning that they preferred the "spiritual" over material things. They also spent a lot of time reading Thoreau and Emerson. Today Diane laughs at the pretense of it all. "I'm sure it was a terribly polluted creek," she recalls.

The Seneca High School yearbook lists very impressive credits under the name of Lila Diane Sawyer. Following the saying "In youth and beauty, wisdom is but rare" is the list of activities: class vice-president, cheerleader, calendar girl, and debating club member, as well as editor in chief of the *Arrow*. The smiling picture shows a composed, contented high school senior, surely a contrast to the "serious philosopher" who read poetry by the banks of a river.

Although Diane felt that she always followed in the shadow of her sister Linda, she says she didn't feel that she was really in competition with her. It was just, Diane says, that Linda was three years older and "I wanted to do everything she did." Call this competition, or normal sibling rivalry, or admiration. Whatever it was, the fact that Linda earned first runner-up in the state Junior Miss contest spurred Diane to enter when she was old enough.

Diane and Linda had much in common. Both were top students, both attended Wellesley College, and both summered in Europe on young people's tours as part of their cultural broadening.

Diane's older sister Linda, shown here at Wellesley College. Even though their lives have taken different directions, the two sisters are still close friends.

Diane recalls her tour. "We were waiting for a train to leave Pisa for Genoa, Italy, when we discovered that some items had been left at the hotel a block away. I made the run back and returned to the train station just as a train was pulling away. I soon discovered that I had boarded the wrong train. My purse, passport, money— everything was on the other train with my group.

"You can imagine my predicament when the conductor asked for my ticket. I could speak no Italian, and he could speak no German or English. Thank heavens for the little German couple who came to my rescue. They loaned me money and acted as my interpreters or I could still be riding the train to and from Pisa and Genoa."

Her ability to think quickly and use the resources available to her, shown in this episode, are among her trademarks as a reporter today.

Both Diane and her sister grew tall, over 5 feet 9 inches. Mrs. Sawyer, surrounded by her two daughters and a husband taller than herself, was sometimes called "Shorty." Says their mother laughingly, "It seems like I have been looking up to Linda and Diane since they were ten years old."

Similar in height, the girls' voices have similarities as well. When they both lived at home, they would mischievously switch places during phone chats. The person at the other end never seemed aware that he or she was talking to two different people.

This similarity of looks, schools, lessons, and voice has led to a continuing closeness for the sisters. Linda's life has taken a different direction from Diane's. She is a marketing director for the Burdine department store chain in Florida and is married with two sons. But even far apart, the two are still good friends and talk often on the phone. Linda's voice carries much of the same enthusiasm heard in Diane's. However, Diane still insists that Linda always did and still can do everything better than she can. Do childhood impressions ever fade?

2

Junior Miss at Wellesley

To Diane Sawyer, her sister Linda may have done everything better than she did. However, Diane did "top" Linda in at least one area, even if she wouldn't say it that way. Linda was runner-up in the Junior Miss pageant. In 1963 Diane won it.

Among other things, winning the Junior Miss pageant meant $11,000 in scholarship money. Certainly she won partly for her looks. Her blond hair was lustrous, and her radiant blue eyes have often been called sapphire. Looks, however, were only part of it. It's said that Diane won for two reasons beyond her looks. One was her poise during the first interview—not bad for someone who called herself intensely shy! The other was for her unusual demonstration of intelligence. The year 1963 was the centennial of the Civil War, and Diane wrote a thoughtful essay comparing the music of the North and South during that conflict.

Diane remembers telling the judges at the Junior Miss interview that she wanted to go into the foreign service when she graduated from college. Actually, at the time she didn't really know what the foreign service was. She'd heard about it in a movie, however, and thought it sounded rather sophisticated and glamorous.

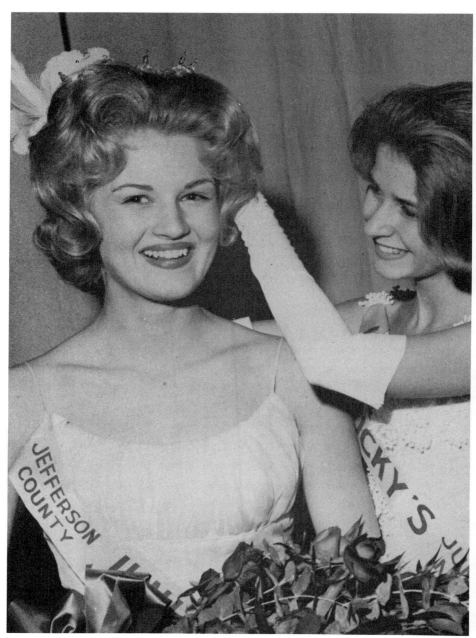

Young Diane is crowned Junior Miss in 1963.

During these teenage years, Diane had other fleeting dreams about what she would do after college. All of her aspirations involved glamour, if not always sophistication.

"As a teenager, I dreamed of being Julie Andrews," she says. "I'd sing along to her records of *The Sound of Music* or *The Boyfriend*." Besides the foreign service and musical comedy, Diane had other career choices. She thought she might like to be a philosopher, although that did not seem very practical. And her third possibility was neither glamorous nor sophisticated, although possibly it was practical. She considered, probably not seriously, becoming a window washer in a garage. "That's because I loved those squirty things that got all the bugs off the windshield," she said. "The task has a nice finite quality to it. You were good at it, and could be pleased."

Diane Sawyer didn't realize any of those youthful dreams. She didn't enter the foreign service, although she certainly has traveled as much as someone in the foreign service might. She has never sung or danced on Broadway, but she has enjoyed the spotlight of a musical comedy star. She isn't known as a philosopher, but she has been able to put her point of view across to people as a philosopher might. Certainly window washing isn't her job, although she has gained the pleasure in a job well done that a good window washer might.

Instead, Diane has become a broadcaster, a very good one, with the glamour and sophistication that goes with that career when you get to the top. And it all can be said to have begun with winning the Junior Miss title in 1963.

Today Diane says that just thinking about the months after she won the pageant makes her "petrified." She was called on to give speeches and travel around the country. Strangely enough, it didn't seem so frightening when she was actually doing it, despite her shyness. She remembers that she just did it. Of course, the speeches and the travel were made a little easier by her chaperone. A woman from Mobile, Alabama, was assigned to travel the country with Diane on her visits as the title holder. Having someone by her side helped to ease her over the rough spots.

The title of America's Junior Miss is awarded for such qualities as poise, talent, fitness, and marks on the SAT college boards. That summer Diane traveled an astounding 25,000 miles, including a visit to New York City. She spoke before groups or boards of corporations as many as three times a day. The pace was hectic, and it didn't help that she was told to wear her crown and sash at all times, even on airplanes!

Even with the frivolous aspects of being Junior Miss and being the only one in an entire airplane wearing a crown, there were benefits. Diane couldn't, of course, have known at the time how helpful all that touring would be in her future career. Learning to think on her feet and to speak without a prepared speech, as she was so often required to do, were great aids in the world of journalism years later.

Although she has called it "an education in terror," Diane did learn that she could stand up in front of hundreds, or even thousands, of people without a script in front of her. She didn't consider her talks "wonderful" or "great," but despite her shyness she found out that she could do it. She wouldn't panic. What a valuable lesson for a future reporter to learn!

The Junior Miss pageant also served to give young Diane Sawyer one of her early role models. In Mobile, Alabama, where the competition was held, she met Catherine Marshall, a well-known writer. Marshall was a pageant judge. Diane remembers the gray eyes of this dignified woman when she asked questions or addressed each of the seventeen-year-olds competing.

The other judges concentrated on asking such things as what the girls would do in certain social situations or what their favorite hobbies were. But Catherine Marshall was different. She thought, Diane recalls, that even seventeen-year-olds, perhaps *especially* seventeen-year-olds, should be encouraged to think about their values and their ambitions in a serious way. With her penetrating eyes and deliberate speech, Marshall held the young women to a more exacting standard.

On the last day of the Junior Miss pageant, Catherine Marshall gathered all the contestants around her. Diane was expecting a rallying pep talk. Instead she received a message that was to change her life.

Marshall said, "You have set goals for yourselves. I have heard some of them. But I don't think you have set them high enough. You have talent and intelligence and a chance. I think you should take those goals and expand them. Think of the most you could do with your lives. Make what you do matter. Above all, dream big."

This kind of talk, the most inspiring of pep talks, became an internal force in Diane's life from then on. She *would* dream big. Catherine Marshall became a mentor to Diane. They corresponded and visited until the older woman's death in 1983. As in the best of mentoring relationships, it was mutually beneficial. After Diane won the Junior Miss contest, Catherine Marshall got her to write an article for the religious magazine Marshall was involved with, called *Guideposts*. And later, when Diane was working with ex-President Richard Nixon for a period of time stretching into years, Marshall asked her a simple question, "What is next?" It forced Diane to reexamine her life's direction and make plans to hold herself to a standard and move on. When Catherine Marshall died, once again Diane Sawyer wrote an article for *Guideposts*, telling of how much the older woman had influenced her life.

With Catherine Marshall's inspiring words at the Junior Miss pageant on her lips and in her heart, young Diane was ready to do the traveling necessary for the crown holder. When the summer tour was finished, she was ready to leave the family nest and head for college, dreaming big every inch along the way.

Diane was off to Wellesley College, her high school diploma

put away, all kinds of lessons tucked into her head, and the Junior Miss crown in her past. Linda was already there, now entering her junior year.

Located in the Massachusetts city whose name it shares, Wellesley College was chartered in 1870. It is approximately twelve miles west-southwest of Boston. Wellesley is one of the so-called Seven Sisters schools, the name given to the group of prestigious colleges in the Northeast that were, at the time, all female. (The other six of the Seven Sisters are Barnard, Bryn Mawr, Mt. Holyoke, Smith, Radcliffe, and Vassar.) Diane attended Wellesley on a scholarship. The school had always been a leader in women's education. Its wooded campus is noted for its beauty, and Wellesley is proud of the fact that it was the country's first women's college to have scientific laboratories.

Life at Wellesley was far different from Louisville or the Junior Miss circuit. In fact, being known as the Junior Miss title holder didn't amount to much in the eyes of Diane's classmates. These intellectual young women weren't impressed with her title at all, which only added to her self-consciousness about it.

Once again Diane's feelings of inferiority came trotting out— this time, though, with a different twist. As Diane tells it, she became consumed with the idea that everyone in the world (or at least on campus) was just hoping for a chance to ridicule her. What's more, she was convinced she would give them that chance if they just waited long enough. It seemed as though the "fame" of being Junior Miss was catching up with her, but in a strange way. She kept imagining that young men would ask her out because she was sort of a celebrity. Then she pictured that after the date they would go back and tell their friends, "Diane Sawyer? Oh, she's not so great."

Taking herself very seriously, Diane spent lots of time worrying that someone was lurking around the corner waiting to trip her up. Surely they would uncover any small trace of snobbish sophistication she might have hidden. Or else she would torment herself with "serious" questions, such as a future philosopher might ask. Questions like "Am I attuned to the spiritual majesty of the universe?"

If anyone at school *did* think Diane was sophisticated or stuck up, such thoughts probably vanished when she began receiving packages from home. She remembers that classmates would get boxes of chocolates and other goodies. But Diane's packages from Louisville were more apt to contain tomatoes or turnips from the family garden. The fruits and vegetables came beautifully wrapped, as she remembers. Actually, she must have known quite a lot about fruits and vegetables, because one of the aptitude tests Diane took at Wellesley suggested that she would make an excellent farmer.

All in all, Diane Sawyer attended Wellesley in much the same way she had gone through Seneca High in Louisville. She was an excellent student with a high grade-point average, in spite of finding time to engage in all sorts of extracurricular activities.

She performed in the Wellesley Junior Show, titled *One Knight's Stand*. She was an actress in on-campus theatrical productions, sang two songs in one show, and was a member of the Wellesley Blue Notes, a choral group. There were no sororities at Wellesley (and still aren't), so Diane could not be a member of a college sisterhood even if she had wanted to be. But this young woman who says she feared that people were trying to expose her as a phony was elected vice-president of the college student body.

Life at Wellesley was the same story as in elementary and high schools—all sorts of achievements and accolades from others, and lots of criticism from herself. It's obvious from her pictures during those teenage years that Diane Sawyer was a very attractive young girl, just as it is obvious today that she is a beautiful woman. To hear Diane tell it, however, you might think she was a horror. In elementary school she complains that in a school ballet her sister was given the part of a snowflake while she played a less graceful icicle. In high school, she laments, "My glasses were an inch thick." (Now she wears contact lenses on camera.) And, according to her recollections, her increasing height made her even clumsier than in the icicle days. She insists that she was always running into glass doors and such. She even claims that she won the Junior Miss title partly for regaining her composure after bumping into things on stage.

In Wellesley the self-criticism continued, and it continues to this day. Diane likes to imagine going back and doing it all different-ly. "I'd study differently, I'd work differently. There are dates I should have turned down, and dates I should have accepted. There

Diane appears in the Wellesley College production of *The Threepenny Opera*.

has been untold carelessness," she says, verbally slapping herself before anyone else can.

Like many a college student, the years at Wellesley were intense times for Diane. She suffered an "identity crisis," taking from a college rich with gifts to bestow and bestowing some of her own back to the college in exchange. In short, these were growing years, as hard for Junior Miss as for anyone else.

Then, in 1967, at the end of four years at Wellesley College, Diane Sawyer graduated with a Bachelor of Arts degree in English. Now what?

Diane hadn't the faintest idea what she wanted to do with her life.

3

On the Air and in the White House

With her spanking new B.A. degree in hand, in 1967 Diane Sawyer returned home to Louisville, where once again she lived with her family. And it was her father who headed her in the direction of a career.

When she asked her father for some inspiration about what she should do with her life after college, he responded with a question. "What is it you enjoy doing most?"

Diane replied, "Writing. I like the power of the word. And working with people. And being in touch with what's happening in the world."

That was when her father suggested that journalism might be a good career for his daughter. A specific, forward-looking type of journalism at that. "Did you ever consider television?" he asked.

Mr. Sawyer's instincts were certainly on target. In 1967 there were hardly any women in television journalism at all.

Diane realized that it would be difficult to break into a field that seemed nearly closed to women. It would mean lots of hard work.

Her father's idea reminded her of Catherine Marshall's edict to "dream big."

Okay, she said to herself, I *will* dream big.

Diane marched herself off in what she decided was a Mary Tyler Moore "girl-journalist" suit, prepared to talk her way into one of the first "women in journalism" jobs. And so she did. The news director at Louisville WLKY-TV, a local ABC station, hired her even though she had no experience. She was to be a "weathergirl" and a part-time reporter.

"Weather is nature, weather is change," she said, launching her channel 32 career. Although it wasn't exactly what she had in mind, Diane had respect for the importance of weather. She said, "People tune in to see what they'll be able to do because weather affects what they wear, their morale, and just about every part of their lives."

Ever looking at herself as inadequate, Diane thought her lack of meteorology background would lead to dull weather reports. So she spiced them up (and made herself more comfortable along the way) by adding appropriate lines of poetry to demonstrate the day's weather. "A little Emily Dickinson, a little Baudelaire. Whoever was handy."

There were a few bloopers, common to all weather forecasters, Diane recalls. One night she ended her segment with "It'll be colder and warmer tomorrow." On another occasion she announced, "The high today was forty-nine degrees and the present temperature is fifty-one."

"I was a terrible weathergirl," Sawyer remembers. "I was so bad at it." Besides her lack of a meteorology background, Diane's other problem with weather reporting was her eyesight. Her uncorrected vision is about 20/400 (20/20 is considered normal). She still wore glasses, but she didn't wear them on camera. She recalls that when she stood in front of the weather map back in Louisville, she didn't know if she was looking at the East Coast or the West Coast!

Diane Sawyer's Wellesley College yearbook picture.

Besides that, she just wasn't interested in the weather. She still gets embarrassed when she thinks about those years.

However, even though Diane was unhappy with weather reporting, she did gain valuable experience during that period. Sometimes she and a camera crew were sent out into the city to do "on-the-spot" forecasts and news stories.

Recalls Sawyer, "The first time I went out to shoot film I was a day late for the assignment. The second time it was all jerks and knots. My third try was on a hike through the Red River Gorge. I had to stand ahead of the hikers, then stand and shoot until they passed by, then race ahead to be in front of them again. It was really a vigorous hike for me."

Diane did learn a lot about her craft during her time in Louisville. Obviously television was the right place for her. A shy person, she appeared transformed and composed on the television screen. Aside from the occasional blooper at the weather map, in general she seemed calm and self-assured. These are wonderful traits for a television broadcaster to possess. And few people worked harder trying to be better.

Diane realized that she needed more training and experience before she could really break into news reporting. But that didn't stop her from tormenting the station officials for more interesting work. Eventually her persistence and hard work paid off. She was promoted to a full-time correspondent for news.

Although she worked on many different stories and began to meet many important people, one of her first assignments is the one she remembers best. She was sent out to get an interview with Supreme Court Justice William O. Douglas. This renowned civil rights supporter served on the U.S. Supreme Court longer than any other justice, from 1939 to 1975.

The only way Diane could get an interview with the busy justice was to follow him on a five-mile hike through eastern Kentucky's Red River Gorge. That particular stretch of wilderness is very

"Weathergirl" Sawyer at work back in Louisville.

rugged, and Diane had to carry her own camera and equipment. Her memory of that trek is that she wasn't a very good newswoman. But she did get the interview.

Diane took a semester of law courses at the university while she was in Louisville. For a time, especially when she seemed to be getting nowhere in broadcasting, she considered a law career and a life similar to her father's. But as she gained experience in news reporting and got better and better assignments, she knew that a law career was not for her.

In 1969, while Diane was still working at station WLKY, she and her family suffered a terrible loss. Her beloved father was killed in an auto crash. He was driving to work one very early morning and, mysteriously, crashed his car into an abutment. It is thought that he might have been distracted by answering the intercom telephone in his official county car.

Diane's sorrow was great. She says that her father was the center of their family life. In assessing his influence on her, Sawyer refers to the novel *The Unbearable Lightness of Being*. "Milan Kundera says you can judge people by the eyes that they feel on them. Actors and actresses like the feeling of anonymous eyes. Then there are people who mainly like the feeling of all eyes in the room. Then there are the people who want to have the eyes—and the love—of only one other person. But finally there are the people who feel the need for unseen eyes. While my father was alive, he was the reference point, the center of gravity in our family; after he died, he became the unseen eyes."

Judge Sawyer was highly respected in Louisville. A memorial to him stands in town in E. P. "Tom" Sawyer Park. The people of his city believe that a place where trees and flowers grow, where sun shines and children swing and laugh, is a very suitable memorial to one of its beloved citizens.

It took some time for the family to pull itself together after Judge Sawyer's death. Mrs. Doris Waddel, family friend, said,

"They were very disciplined people. They were in the habit of doing what they were supposed to do, and they just picked up and went on." Diane's mother has since remarried and still lives in Louisville. Both daughters were very happy with the remarriage, and the family remains close.

A year after her father's death, Diane decided to leave Louisville for the larger world of Washington, D.C. "I was looking for an intellectual vitamin," she says. "I began to feel restless. I'd lie awake at night feeling that something wasn't right. I'd wait for the revelation, the sign pointing in the direction of the Big Dream. What I didn't realize is what Catherine Marshall undoubtedly knew all along—that the dream is not the destination but the journey."

Her father's death had been a factor in spurring her interest in continuing on the journey. His death had also ignited further interest in government and politics. She knew that she didn't want to stay in Louisville. So she tried to think of what she could and should do next, racking her brain for ideas. She asked others for ideas, too. Once again, a good idea came in the form of a question. Her father had asked, "What do you like to do best?" A family friend, one of her father's associates, asked, "What about Washington?"

The decision was made. Diane would leave her hometown for the nation's capital. It was at that time, she recalls, that she really understood what a wonderful gift her mother had given her. She was able to go, says Diane, without feeling any guilt about leaving the family.

But why Washington? It seemed right to her for several reasons. It was a beautiful city and she thought she would like living there. It was the center of politics, which Diane found herself increasingly enjoying. And it didn't seem as frightening as did New York City.

The first thing Diane did in Washington was to visit all the television stations in the area in search of work. Although she felt that she was ready for "bigger things" in the field of broadcasting, the sophisticated journalism world in the nation's capital did not seem overly impressed with the young reporter from Kentucky.

An exception was the Washington bureau chief for CBS, Bill Small. He remembered Diane's family from when he had worked in Louisville and had admiration for them. Small met with Diane, and he was smart enough to see her potential. He wanted to hire her. But there was a freeze on hiring new people at CBS. So Small told her to be patient and wait. He would hire her when he could.

But Diane wasn't one to simply wait for better things to happen to her. She was going to make them happen herself. And often her "quiet persistence" paid off. So did, as she later said, the fact that she had "chosen her parents wisely."

Diane Sawyer has written that her impulse to work at the White House was with her at the time of her arrival. "Now I know this may sound incredibly naive, but when the plane landed at National Airport, I got off with a very firm idea of where I wanted to work. At the White House. True, in the eyes of official Washington I might be right off the equivalent of the turnip truck, but working in the White House was exactly what I had in mind!"

It doesn't matter whether broadcasting was her first desire and this White House plan became first choice when broadcasting wasn't available, or whether broadcasting from the White House was really the goal. What does matter is that Diane succeeded in getting herself work at the White House. Her father's career as a Republican judge back in Kentucky had given him contacts with important Republicans in the nation's capital. Now one of these contacts advised her to "pop in" at the White House, at that time under the Republican banner of Richard Nixon. She did. The friend's recommendation was enough for her to obtain an interview with Ron Ziegler, the White House press secretary for President Nixon. It was Ziegler's job to deal with all the newspaper, radio, and TV reporters. The press secretary explained events, made announcements, and served as a go-between so the president wouldn't be constantly bombarded with questions and requests.

Ziegler, like Bill Small from CBS, knew a good thing when he saw it, and he hired Diane Sawyer. Always knocking herself, Sawyer later said that she was sure Ziegler had been flooded with phone calls on her behalf. Many of Diane's father's friends and colleagues were trying to help her land a job in the White House.

Ziegler remembers that Diane was very "detail oriented" and had great ability to do her job. She was made an assistant to Jerry Warren, the White House deputy press secretary.

The White House, where Diane worked during the administration of Richard M. Nixon.

From the start of her time in the White House, Diane did tasks that could have important consequences, such as writing press releases. She was promoted quickly to even more demanding work, such as drafting some of the president's public statements.

Diane's first actual meeting with President Nixon occurred just a few weeks after she joined the White House staff. It was hardly a formal introduction and certainly not the way you would imagine meeting the president of the United States. Diane nearly knocked him down. She ran right into the president when she was trotting briskly down a hallway in the White House, a pair of scissors in her hand. Nixon fell backward, and two of the Secret Service men who guard the president had to catch him. However, he didn't seem bothered by the run-in. "You could get hurt this way," he cheerfully told Diane when she quickly began to apologize.

In less than a year, Diane Sawyer was promoted to Ziegler's administrative assistant, a position of importance on the White House staff. From there she made the big move—to staff assistant to Richard Milhous Nixon, the president of the United States.

Diane was now sitting beside the nation's seat of power. It seemed as though her career could hardly get better. Little did she know that the Nixon administration and all those connected with it were about to become embroiled in a period of great turmoil, a period that would upset the country and end in personal disgrace for the president. This period of American history is known as the Watergate affair. It began in 1972 with a break-in at Democratic headquarters (in the Watergate building) in Washington D.C. It ended in 1974 with President Nixon's announcement of resignation.

Anyone watching television on the day President Nixon resigned and boarded a plane for his home in San Clemente, California, could have seen a tall, attractive woman in the background. Intensely loyal to the president, Diane Sawyer was one of the small number of aides who went to San Clemente with him to organize some of the Watergate materials.

Diane planned to stay at San Clemente for one month. She stayed four years.

Why did she go in the first place? Why did she stay so long? In answer to both questions, Diane replies, "I am by nature loyal." She continues: "I had worked for this man, and he had been good to me. Now he was asking me for something I was in a position to give. I have never regretted the decision. I stayed."

Diane Sawyer has been criticized for her loyalty to President Nixon, and her involvement with the Watergate affair did put obstacles in her career path. Today she is careful to steer clear of partisan politics. She does not talk much about the Nixon years. But as a young staff assistant in the White House back in the early 1970s, Diane could scarcely have known what a different course her career would take when she first heard the word *Watergate*.

4

Watergate

The so-called Watergate affair or Watergate scandal (1972–1974) was a sad, disrupting chapter in the history of the United States. It ruined the careers of many people in very high places in American politics and government. In fact, Watergate went to the very top. For no one held a higher position or was more affected by the scandal than Richard Nixon, thirty-seventh president of the United States.

Nixon had become part of the federal government back in 1946 when he was elected to the House of Representatives. Before very long this young Republican from California made a name for himself. A government official named Alger Hiss was suspected of being a Russian spy. Nixon played a key role in the investigation that followed. During the trial, Nixon accused the Democratic party of being "soft on communism." His tough stand made him enemies. Many people later accused him of rough tactics when he criticized the well-liked Senator (1949–1973) Margaret Chase Smith of Maine. Or when he sided with Senator Joseph McCarthy in harassing Americans whom McCarthy accused of being "Reds" (or

Communists). Young Nixon may not always have been liked, but he did seem always to be in the public eye.

In 1951 Nixon ran for the Senate. His opponent was Helen Gahagan Douglas, wife of movie star Melvyn Douglas. During the campaign Nixon made comments that seemed to accuse Helen Douglas of leaning toward communism. This was the height of the so-called Cold War, the unfriendly state of affairs between the Soviet Union and the United States. Many Americans were very much afraid of communism. Whether or not that was the reason, Nixon won election to the Senate, and also more criticism along the way.

The next year Richard Nixon took an even bigger step. In 1952 he was elected vice-president of the United States on the Republican ticket with Dwight D. Eisenhower. Nixon and the popular "Ike" were reelected in 1956.

Now one of the country's most prominent figures, Nixon ran for the presidency himself in 1960. He lost in a very close race to Democrat John F. Kennedy. Four years later he lost again; this time in the race for the governorship of California. It was a low period for Nixon. Critics said his career was over. How wrong they were!

Richard Nixon was determined to become president. He gave it one more try, and this time he won. He defeated Hubert Humphrey in 1968 with a little more than 43 percent of the popular vote.

During his first presidential term, the Watergate scandal began. However, in spite of growing suspicions that Nixon was involved somehow in Watergate, he was easily reelected for a second term in 1972. Nixon swamped his Democratic opponent, George McGovern, this time with more than 60 percent of the popular vote.

When Diane Sawyer joined the White House staff, President Nixon was about halfway through his first term in office. He was at the height of his career and power. Things couldn't be going better.

Then came Watergate.

44

Just what was Watergate? Just what happened to bring down a man who held one of the two most important and powerful jobs in the world (the other being the head of the Soviet Union)?

Watergate is a luxury apartment building, hotel, and office complex in Washington, D.C. Its name has become synonymous with "dirty dealings" in government. What happened at Watergate was a break-in. Early in the morning of June 17, 1972, five men were arrested in the Watergate building. They had broken into the Democratic national headquarters on the sixth floor. These were the

Shown here before the Watergate troubles began, President Nixon stands behind his desk and jokes with the press.

Democratic headquarters for the election campaign that would be run against Nixon in the fall. The "burglars" were wearing surgical gloves so they wouldn't leave fingerprints, and they were carrying electronic gear. It looked as though they were trying to tap the telephones.

At first the newspapers and most of the people in Washington treated the Watergate break-in as a joke. What was there to steal at the Democratic headquarters after all? What could they possibly be after? Did they want to steal information from the Democrats? That seemed funny, especially since all the polls were predicting a landslide victory for Nixon.

The laughter may have been loud, but it didn't last long. The men who broke into the Watergate were tried and convicted in 1973, after Nixon was reelected. The convictions opened the floodgates, and all sorts of information came tumbling out.

The reasons behind the actual break-in were not world-shattering. Some members of the Nixon reelection campaign committee simply wanted to tap the telephones in the Democrats' headquarters. If they could listen in to the Democratic conversations, they thought that perhaps they would have the upper hand when election time came around. They were also looking for papers that would show how much the Democrats knew about campaign funds that had been contributed to Nixon's reelection campaign. Of course, the break-in was illegal, but all by itself it wasn't world-shattering.

What happened *after* Watergate, however, turned out to be world-shattering indeed!

If the five men had not been caught at the Watergate, that might have been the end of the story. But they *were* caught. And all kinds of facts began to be uncovered. Each day there seemed to be new stories, stories about illegal spying and hidden funds of money and corrupt activities at all levels of government. It was as though a *"simple"* break-in had become the key to unlocking a whole room full of illegal activities.

For example, one of the convicted burglars wrote a letter to the judge who had tried the Watergate case. The letter said that people in very high places in government were trying to cover up what had happened at the Democratic headquarters. After that letter, the troubles for the Nixon administration really began.

Watergate erupted into a national scandal. President Nixon got himself into trouble from the very start. He kept telling the American people that he knew nothing about the Watergate events. He kept repeating that no one in his administration had been involved

Following a president around can be a hectic life. President Nixon is shown here with reporters in tow.

in the break-in. What's more, the president said, if anyone *had* been involved, he'd find out about it.

In February 1973 the Senate voted to establish a committee to investigate the now growing Watergate affair. More and more people were dragged into the scandal. In April the president's top White House aides, H. R. Haldeman and John Ehrlichman, resigned. The president stubbornly stuck to his story: no one was involved with covering up the Watergate scandal, and he didn't know anything about it.

But the Senate committee kept finding out more and more about secret money funds and other undercover activities. The more the committee found out, the more the president denied. In May he went on television to tell the American people that he knew nothing of the burglary or the attempts to cover it up.

At first, Americans seemed willing to believe the president. At least they seemed willing to forgive him if he had known anything about what happened.

Yet, as Nixon kept saying he knew nothing and more and more scandal was uncovered, the public grew more and more suspicious. Nixon's popularity began to drop, and it kept on dropping.

Things were also going badly for Nixon at the Senate investigation hearings. In June the president's counsel, John Dean, took the stand and publicly accused Nixon of being involved in Watergate. The next month another bombshell exploded. A former White House aide, Alexander Butterfield, told the Senate committee there was a secret taping system in the White House. Butterfield said that the president had been secretly recording conversations in his office for a long time. People who went in to talk to the president usually didn't know that their conversations were being recorded, said Butterfield.

Of course, it wasn't illegal for the president to tape his telephone conversations, although it did seem unethical to many that he didn't tell most of his visitors that they were being recorded.

However, the committee reasoned that listening to the tapes would clear up the question of just how much the president knew about Watergate, and when. So they asked to see the tapes. The president refused. He said they were his private property and were intended for his use only when he wrote his memoirs in later years.

The fight over the Senate's right to hear the tapes and the president's right to privacy went back and forth. Finally it went all the way to the United States Court of Appeals. The court ruled that the White House must turn over the tapes to the Senate committee.

As if the president didn't have enough problems at this point, he was hit with more trouble. On October 10 his vice-president, Spiro T. Agnew, resigned. He was charged with corrupt practices in the state of Maryland, where he had been governor before Nixon chose him as a running mate. Two days later the president named Congressman Gerald R. Ford of Michigan as the new vice-president.

In this change of office Ford became the first nonelected vice-president in our nation's history. In 1967 the Twenty-fifth Amendment to the U.S. Constitution had been passed. It said that whenever the office of vice-president became vacant—as when Agnew resigned—the president was to nominate someone to fill the post. Before that time, if a vacancy occurred, the office was not to be filled until the next election.

Meanwhile, the Senate investigators now had the Nixon tapes. They soon discovered that some of the tapes were missing, and parts of tapes had been erased. Things began to look bleaker than ever for the president. Privately some of his aides began to urge him to resign. Nixon refused.

During this period, Diane Sawyer was asked by someone if the president was thinking of resigning. "Wouldn't you be?" she replied.

Whatever the president was thinking and feeling, he tried to act as though everything was normal. Business at the White House went on as usual during the next few months. In June 1974, while rumors flew that he would leave office, the president visited the Middle East. From there he went to the Soviet Union for an important summit meeting.

In July President Nixon returned home. Soon he learned of the news he most dreaded to hear. The House of Representatives, on July 17, 1974, passed the first article of impeachment against Nixon concerning his involvement in the Watergate scandal.

Impeachment means an attempt by a legislature to remove a

Diane and fellow journalists on a trip to China.

public official from office. In the United States, the House of Representatives is the body that brings the articles of impeachment against an official, and the Senate is the body that brings the official to trial. The word loosely covers two things: both the bringing of the charges (by the House) and the trial itself (by the Senate). A president of the United States has been impeached only once in our history. In 1868 Andrew Johnson, seventeenth president of the United States, was accused of trying to force his secretary of war out of office. But the Senate failed to convict Johnson by one vote.

By the end of July the House had passed its third and final article of impeachment. The next step would be the trial by the Senate.

There was no trial, however. On August 8, 1974, Nixon went on television before the American public and tearfully resigned the office of president of the United States. He was the first ever to do so.

Officially, Richard M. Nixon resigned on August 9, 1974. That same day Gerald R. Ford became the thirty-eighth (and first non-elected) president of the United States.

One month later President Ford pardoned Nixon for his part in the Watergate affair. When Ford ran for the presidency in 1976, he lost a close race to Jimmy Carter. Many say that a large part of that defeat was due to the pardon.

There were many unanswered questions about Watergate, and there still are. But that sad episode in American history had finally come to an end. Nixon returned to his home in San Clemente, California, to pick up the pieces of his life. One of the things he wanted most to do was to organize all the written materials of his presidency. To help in that project, certain aides went along on that plane to San Clemente. Diane Sawyer was one of them.

5

California and the Road Back

During Watergate, Diane Sawyer became known, as on earlier jobs, for her tireless work schedule. ''The [White House] guards told me I had the longest hours at the White House,'' she says. Because she was determined to try to understand Watergate, she would usually get to work before six A.M. and often wouldn't leave until ten P.M. Not surprisingly, she became somewhat of a Watergate expert.

Besides keeping track of the actual events of the scandal, Diane oversaw media coverage as well. In fact, some Washington reporters said they observed her growing loyalty to the president. Because of it, they said, she sometimes tried to persuade them not to publish or broadcast information that might be damaging to Nixon. Dan Rather, CBS anchorman, recalls that Diane was so close-mouthed ''she was a total nonsource, close to the cuff.'' However, at the same time Rather says, ''She was very competent about her job, and if you needed a statistic or a spelling at the last minute, she was always the one you went to.''

When Nixon resigned, Ron Ziegler asked Diane if she would join the team of about eight journalists going with him to San

Clemente. Diane knew she would be putting herself in exile right along with the president, but she didn't hesitate. She says it was "out of a sense of what was honorable."

She continues: "It was a human consideration. Here was a man whose dreams were shattered. If I didn't come through for him at a time when he needed me, I couldn't have lived with myself. . . . Here was a man who, in better times, had given me a ringside seat to a lot of history. But it wasn't just gratitude. When someone's dreams have shattered around him, and he asks you for help, what kind of person would you be if you said no?"

Diane's life changed dramatically when she accompanied the former president to the relative quiet of San Clemente, California.

Diane says that, also, she had grown attached to the people who were working in the White House at that time. She adds that she is politically independent; in other words, she would have been just as happy working for a Democrat. She admired the good goals that the White House people were working toward at the time. In fact, when she looks back today, she sometimes thinks about "what might have been." How impressive the Nixon presidency could have been without Watergate, she muses, especially in foreign relations where Nixon opened up talks with China and warmed up the Cold War with the Soviet Union.

Diane Sawyer also had another feeling about going to San Clemente. She felt it would be a unique opportunity to be part of history as this president tried to rebuild his life. "What could be more stimulating than to sit with the man who is the political continuity of my generation?" she asks. "To watch him reconstruct his life and search through the past to examine the way it defined his destiny, to hear him talk about the people he met, the difference they made, and the difference they might have made. It was taxing, it was exhausting, and it was a graduate education to exceed any other."

As an expert on Watergate, Diane intended to stay at San Clemente just long enough to organize the enormous files on the subject. She stayed for four years.

"Nixon was considerate and observant, and I stayed for four years because it was a compelling project," she explains.

Diane recalls that immediate post-Watergate period as very confused. After the pardon, Nixon was ill for a time. At first, her job was as part of the team that would help to make the transition from the Nixon to the Ford administration. This was not, of course, easy under the circumstances. And even though Diane had been at San Clemente (the so-called Summer White House) before, this time it was in a way very strange. When Nixon was president, at San Clemente one walked into the chaos of Marine guards patrolling the complex and the constant noise of jangling telephones and buzzing helicopters overhead. Now it was all quiet. Too quiet. Only a few guards patrolled the area; the telephones often did not ring for long periods.

One of Diane's responsibilities during the post-Watergate stay was to intercept phone calls from reporters. To anyone seeking a story, she said, "There is no news. This is no longer a public operation." However, she was very aware of the mixed sentiments the public held about her boss. Once she pointed to two boxes of mail. The big one contained good wishes and get well cards. The other was filled with "drop dead letters."

In time Diane and the rest of the staff adjusted to this new, quieter atmosphere. Now Diane went on to her next task—organizing the Watergate files. Then she became Nixon's research assistant. Along with Frank Gannon, White House staff member, and Ken Khachigian, speech writer, she would help Nixon write his autobiography, entitled *RN*.

The three members of the research team each focused on one part of the book. For Diane, it was, of course, Watergate. By that time she was a leading expert on the whole affair. Over time she would know even more.

"I went over everything. I went over the newspaper clippings. I read every book extant on Watergate, and books written by any of the participants. I reread all of the [U.S. Senator Sam] Ervin Committee hearing books. I cross-referenced everything. I had the definitive cross-reference dictionary of Watergate. Everything that I could think of, everything that was on the public record, I read through and reorganized in a cross-referenced, chronological book of my own." Diane also conducted interviews with many of the participants in the events of those times, even visiting Ehrlichman in prison, adding information to her book.

The "book" that resulted contained a "flow chart," which traced, day-by-day, events in the Watergate affair and established links between the personalities involved. When Nixon saw Sawyer's document in late July 1977, he read it for a time, then looked up. Taking off his reading glasses, he exclaimed, "You know, this is the first time I've really understood everything that happened."

Besides putting together the information that was already available in print or from interviews, Diane interviewed the former president himself. She acted as the interrogator for his memoirs, asking probing questions.

Sawyer's interviews with Nixon were held at regular times and sometimes lasted five or six hours. They took place in the living room, as the sun set over San Clemente. Diane recalls, "Sometimes the talks would be breathtakingly personal. He used conversation as relaxation and a way of making decisions—that's why the tapes were so long—so anyone listening became a sounding board. The oddest part was that he had had all those resources, and suddenly there were only the three of us. We were his conduits."

The decision was made to tackle the memoirs in chronological order. In this way, it was hoped that Nixon would come to see that Watergate had not been a sudden surprise but rather a more direct result of other themes in his life. Yet, when it was completed, even with Diane's document as a jumping-off point, the Watergate material had to be dragged out of Nixon. As a result, the book has been criticized as hardly revealing.

Some people wonder why Diane Sawyer didn't become disillusioned just reading about Watergate. Some ask why she wasn't disheartened by the sheer load of material she was amassing. Or by Nixon's still guarded replies about Watergate when he was so open about so many other subjects. To such questions, Diane replies that she felt her eyes were open and she was forthright in describing the negative side of Richard Nixon. "I just felt this monumental sense of responsibility not to let mistakes be made in the book. I didn't want to add to the public's cynicism by having the book undermined with factual errors."

If Nixon didn't disclose much about Watergate in his book, Diane doesn't look at it as a failure on her part. It wasn't the job of the editors, researchers, or writers to force material out of him, she says. "None of us lured him into an unconsidered confession or admission. I think, rather, that our job—and we did it well—was, through our own distance and detachment, to help him see the patterns of his life."

Nixon is perhaps not an easy man to know. Although Diane spent long exhausting hours with him, sometimes hearing some of his most intimate thoughts, their relationship remained formal. She always addressed him as "Mr. President," as did the other assistants. But life among the assistants was neither formal nor dull. In fact, she and Frank Gannon were thought to be "romantically linked." They would spend tiring, full days at the San Clemente complex, then try to unwind during the evenings at the theater or movies. She remembers *The Rocky Horror Picture Show* as a favorite. Diane says they would enter the movie house and try to put everything else out of their minds, "to pretend that they still had a youth."

It was an exhausting, once-in-a-lifetime experience. Diane felt that she "learned a great deal about self-discipline and self-renewal" and that she "came to appreciate the way in which experience hones perception."

In time, however, work on the memoirs was at its end. Was Diane frightened about looking for work again? "There must be something wrong with me," she has said, "but I don't remember being frightened about prospects." She may have been a bit like Rip Van Winkle trying to get back to the "outside" world of journalism, but she says, "it never occurred to me that something wouldn't develop."

One the eve of finishing the book, Sawyer and Gannon were

packing the manuscript pages into boxes for the typesetter. Nixon entered the room. "I guess this calls for a celebration," he said.

Nixon opened a bottle of brandy and poured them all drinks. This was very special brandy, he announced, and he had opened it only twice before. The first time was with Henry Kissinger, Nixon's secretary of state. That had marked the end of negotiations for the trip that would open up relations with China. The second time was the ex-president's last night in the White House. In a quiet but emotional toast, he thanked the team "for all they had done for him, the good work they had accomplished together." Then he said, "To the book. To the future."

It was done. Everyone involved was worn out.

Diane and Frank Gannon vacationed in Hawaii, and then both returned to Washington, D.C. Frank was going to join the staff of a Pennsylvania senator; Diane was going to CBS. (Frank Gannon has worked as a producer for the David Letterman show on NBC.)

Diane Sawyer had boarded a plane for San Clemente when she was twenty-eight years old. Now she was thirty-two and back in the nation's capital. However, the four years had cost her more than just time. Most of her fellow journalists were not glad to see her. To Diane the period in San Clemente may have been a once-in-a-lifetime opportunity, but to her colleagues she was "marked" by Watergate even if not involved in it.

Yet all was not bad news, for Bill Small, who years before had wanted to hire Diane but was stopped by a job freeze, stepped in with an offer. Small was now a senior vice-president in the CBS News division. For some time now he had been trying to get Diane out of San Clemente. He would send notes saying, "Whenever you're ready to come back in the real world, I have a job for you."

And so he did. Small hired Diane as a general assignment reporter with the CBS News Washington bureau. She recalls that it took some courage for him to insist on giving her a job back then. Certainly no one else at CBS was very happy about it. Some reporters remembered how she had tried to keep them from probing too deeply during the Watergate crisis. Dan Rather even said that Diane had "no credibility" because of her White House involvement. (Rather would later admit to being wrong about Diane. Others never did take back their words but later claimed that they "discovered" her.)

Diane was certainly far too smart not to know what people were thinking. She worked hard to bring people over to her side. Once again, she used the skills that were a natural part of her—diligent work habits, great stamina, attention to detail, intelligence, and the ability to articulate and write clear, to-the-point reports. To win the affection of her new coworkers, she gladly worked weekends and holidays. As in Louisville, once again she spent many a dreary hour on the worst assignments, such as being called out in the middle of the night for long stakeouts waiting for a news story to break.

It wasn't easy. But slowly Diane Sawyer began the climb back. Slowly, too, she won over her critics and became one of their peers.

Diane Sawyer is living proof that hard work can pay off! For, interestingly, it was her willingness to take the less desirable assignments that eventually brought her greater notice. For instance, she gave up her Thanksgiving holiday to be at Dover Air Force Base waiting for bodies from Jonestown, Guyana, to be returned to the United States. (American cult leader Jim Jones had encouraged an entire community of his followers in this small South American country to commit suicide together.) Assignments such as this gave Diane valuable exposure on national television.

Within a year and a half Diane was promoted to correspondent. This came largely as the result of another assignment—Three Mile Island. In March 1979 the cooling system failed in a reactor at the Three Mile Island nuclear power plant near Harrisburg, Pennsylvania. At first there were fears of a nuclear explosion. Thousands of people had to quickly evacuate, leaving their homes and possessions behind. Radioactive gasses were released into the air. The twelve-day crisis at Three Mile Island, which Diane covered with clear, concise reporting, made many Americans sit up and take notice. They were made more aware of nuclear power and grew increasingly fearful of its potential for disaster. The Three Mile Island episode slowed the construction of other nuclear power plants all over the country.

Six months after her promotion, Diane was given the State Department beat. Now her reports showed up regularly on the *CBS*

Diane is shown here at work during the 1980 Democratic convention.

Morning News program. Her face was becoming familiar to millions of Americans.

More and more, Diane became known for covering one particular story—the Iranian hostage crisis. American hostages were being held by Islamic fundamentalists at the United States Embassy in Teheran, Iran, in the Middle East. The State Department was trying to free them, without much success. As on so many assignments before, Diane showed tremendous stamina.

During that crisis she once spent a week at the State Department. She slept only an hour or two when she could steal the time, propped up on two chairs. She was tireless at the telephones, nabbing up-to-the-minute interviews with government officials and the families of the hostages. She always seemed to be on television—in the morning, sometimes in the evening, and from time to time on the CBS News *Sunday Morning* show.

Diane was also becoming almost a regular on the weekday news program with Charles Kuralt. After her reports, she and Kuralt would carry on informal discussions about the news. These conversations began to be noticed because they were filled with references to history and literature (remember the weathergirl poetry!). Many viewers and critics welcomed these rich, meaty discussions as a wonderful contrast to the "happy talk" with little content that many broadcasts delight in.

One of the people who noticed Diane's knowledge and ease before the camera was Mike Wallace. He was one of the early correspondents on *60 Minutes*. "I was mesmerized by her knowledge of the beat," he said, "by her capacity to synthesize information in a remarkably illuminating way. You're given two minutes to tell an important story, all the work you've done all those months has got to be reflected somehow in that. . . . [I thought to myself] . . . this woman knows what she's about."

Diane had come a long way. She had put the Watergate break-in behind her. Now she was ready for her biggest opportunity yet.

6

Mornings with CBS

Diane was doing well as a CBS correspondent and a regular on the *Sunday Morning* show. Then a big break came in 1981. Now thirty-five years old, Diane was no longer the untried newcomer in the world of broadcast news. Other people besides the audience had been watching her work. The heads of the CBS network were impressed, too. In fact, they were impressed enough to make her coanchor of the newly expanded and renamed program *Morning with Charles Kuralt and Diane Sawyer*. It became known by its shorter name, *Morning*. The assignment meant moving to New York City. However, the thought of living in the Big Apple no longer frightened Diane as it had years before.

Charles Kuralt was already a well-established television personality. CBS officials were pleased with the way he and Diane had worked together when she frequently appeared on *Sunday Morning*. They had especially liked her reports during the Iran crisis. So when in early 1981 they decided to expand the morning show from sixty to ninety minutes, Diane seemed a good coanchor choice. Kuralt and Sawyer began to work as a team on September 28, 1981.

Good as Kuralt and Sawyer were together, CBS knew it wasn't

going to be easy. The network had long had trouble with the "breakfast" show spot. Although CBS was strong with the dinner hour news, it just couldn't seem to compete in the mornings. The opponents—the *Today* show on NBC and *Good Morning America* on ABC—were just too strong. CBS used fifteen different anchorpersons over a twenty-seven-year period! Nothing worked. The ratings didn't budge. Now CBS thought it had the answer in the appealing combination of Charles Kuralt and Diane Sawyer.

Of course, Diane had been on television many times before. But this was a brand-new world. She was thrown into one of the most difficult of all jobs on televsion—appearing daily and appearing live. As she recalls, "I had a half hour of exquisite agony two days before the first broadcast. But then it passed."

Within a year, *Morning* had risen by 30 percent in number of viewers. It still remained third among the networks for that spot, but at least it now had a respectable audience share.

Much of the credit for the show's success at that point went to its two stars. The calm, unruffled Kuralt was well liked by audiences and easy to take in the morning. The wit, warmth, and obvious journalistic talents of Diane Sawyer suited him well. The *Morning* reporting team relied on skill and professionalism rather than expensive sets and electronic gadgets.

Another reason for the show's success was that Diane refused to do the so-called soft stories that were often given to female correspondents. "Soft" stories include fashion, human interest, and other features that can be inserted to fill in at any time. Instead, she continued with her on-the-scene coverage of news stories and hard-hitting interviews.

One of Diane's most memorable interviews involved her one-time boss, former President Richard M. Nixon. The occasion was the upcoming tenth anniversary of the Watergate break-in. Diane herself had extended the invitation for the interview. Nixon had accepted, and also invited her to dinner afterward.

The interview was important to Diane not only because of the subject. It was also important because it showed how objective she could be as a reporter after being so involved with a political figure.

The interview started off well and warmly, a reunion of sorts, perhaps two old friends getting together. They talked of many things. But when the talk turned to the press and Watergate, there were some tough exchanges. A few examples follow.

Sawyer asked what Watergate now meant to him. Nixon replied, "It happened a long time ago. I've said everything I can on the subject. I have nothing to add, and I'm looking to the future rather than the past. . . . Never look back."

Sawyer wasn't satisfied. "But a lot of people say, and these are common people, ordinary people, people in the street, say that you never just said, 'I covered up and I'm sorry.' "

"Well, that—is, of course, not true," Nixon came back, apparently now upset. "As a matter of fact, if you—if you go back and . . . read my memoirs, I've covered all that in great, great detail. And I've said it all, and I'm not going to say anything more in the future."

Sawyer pressed on. "Do you think about it when you're just sitting alone?"

"Never," was the snappish reply. "No. If I were thinking about it, I wouldn't be able to—do I—what is some of the constructive work I've been doing on my new books, and also preparing for the travels I'm going to be doing. . . . I'm not going to spend my time just looking back and wringing my hands about something I can't do anything about."

This was still not enough for Sawyer. "You don't even sit sometimes and think to yourself, once again, as everyone thinks you must, 'Why didn't I burn those tapes?' "

"I've covered that also, of course, in my—in my memoirs, and I must say that if—I must get—I must get a—oh, a half a dozen letters a week even now. 'Why didn't you burn those tapes?' And the answer is, of course, I should. It should have been done. But the main part is, they should never have been started."

After the Nixon interview, Diane was asked if she were as rough on the former president as another reporter might have been. "Rougher," she replied. She went on to explain that it troubled her afterward. "It was a very tough interview, with a whole section of Watergate questions, and I wondered in the end if I was overcompensating in some subconscious way. I don't know. You never know those things."

When she was asked if Nixon thought the interview was tough, she answered, "Yeah. I think he did."

Perhaps so. When Diane returned to her office after the interview, there was a message for her. The dinner with the former president was off.

However, Nixon and Sawyer have remained on good terms. She says that the word *friends* is not quite proper because Nixon is such a complicated, extraordinary man. She also feels that once someone has been president, it is very hard for that person to have friends in the normal sense of the word. For Nixon, she says, somehow that word is too simple.

Diane does keep in contact, and occasionally she sees Nixon and his wife, who now live in nearby New Jersey. On a lighter note, Diane says that during one telephone conversation Nixon gave her some "lovely advice about my clothes on the air. He said I should always remember that simplicity is better for me."

Interviews and news stories kept Diane busy as coanchor on the national morning television show. It certainly sounds like a glamorous job. But is it?

The answer is yes and no. Let's set the scene.

The audience is watching the television screen. There sits Diane Sawyer in front of the camera. She looks calm, lovely, and unruffled, enjoying herself as she discusses a crisis in the Middle East, gives a sports report, or interviews a diplomat. What could be more professional?

But what the audience isn't seeing is what appears to be total chaos beyond the range of the camera. At least a dozen people are scurrying back and forth as the news goes on. Huge cameras silently trundle by. Makeup people run and slap powder on a suddenly shiny nose before the camera glare finds it. Production assistants run on and off, removing a prop, bringing in new ones. It's a madhouse.

But the professionals such as Diane Sawyer adapt to the mad-

The Spirit of Achievement Award ceremonies, Yeshiva University, New York City.

house, function admirably in it, and even come to have fun doing it.

Another unglamorous side of a coanchor's job involves time. Diane was on the air each weekday morning during that period. Yet her job took much more of her time than those few hours. Her schedule as an anchorperson was tight and tiring.

Each weekday Diane was out of bed between one and two A.M. She was at the CBS studios less than an hour later, taken by limousine. First she tried to exercise for fifteen minutes. Then she settled down in her office to read newspapers. This was a time-consuming task, for she went through the *New York Times, New York Daily News, Wall Street Journal,* and *Washington Post.* She also read any news stories that had come in overnight from the wire services and overseas bureaus.

Then it was time to meet with the news crew. They discussed the morning's show. Who was to be interviewed? What stories were breaking? Who would do what?

Then it was time to write. A program such as *Morning* had staff writers, of course, but Diane and other correspondents often like to do their own writing when they can. Using their own words and phrasing makes the stories more suited to the speakers' style.

Then it was time for makeup and hair styling. Finally, several hours after arriving at the studio, Diane was ready to go before the camera, looking bright-eyed and eager. Indeed, when the audience saw her, she looked as though she had just walked onto the set. It's all part of the job for any good news correspondent.

Completing the morning show, however, did not mean the end of the workday. Diane's days often did not end until about five P.M. (and remember, they began at about one A.M.). After the program there were phone calls to make, meetings to attend, endless interviews to give.

There were rewards for all this hard work, of course. For this busy schedule, Diane was paid very well. Toward the end of her stint on the news show, she was earning $800,000 a year!

Surprisingly as it may seem, Diane says that despite her hectic schedule, she managed to have a private life, too. She went to dinner parties, to the theater. If she planned to go out in the evening, she would leave the station about five P.M. and go home to sleep for an hour or two. She had long ago learned to survive on a few hours' sleep. Every good reporter does. Says Diane, "Amazingly, the longer I go without sleep, the better I apparently look."

Yet even the tireless Diane Sawyer had to have a day off! Friday was Diane's day when she worked on the *Morning* program. Since the show did not air on Saturdays, she pretty much had Friday to herself after the morning program was over. She treasured those days. Having Friday to herself meant getting out of the studio early. As she said at the time, "Everyone knows that at 9:01 A.M. on Friday, they'd better not stand in the studio doorway or I'll mow them down. It's my one free day—I'm off to brunch with a friend, then an afternoon of movies—at least two, sometimes a third—and dinner. Movies are my tranquilizer—it's dark and I don't have to react for a change."

Weekends, too, were to be treasured. She would catch up on sleep, see more movies or plays, attend concerts, shop, read, and cook. The perfectionist in Diane can be seen in some of her hobbies. Take cooking. When she became interested in it, she tried to master a cookbook alphabetically. Thus at one time guests could have come to her house and have nothing on the menu but beet dishes. They were all cooked perfectly, but they were all beets!

Diane's schedule did not allow her much time to fuss about her home. She lived in a lovely, dignified old building on Central Park West in Manhattan. Neighbors in the building say that her apartment resembled a "college dormitory," sparsely furnished and decorated. A rowing machine was the big furniture item in the dining room.

"I don't care about things," says Diane. The only luxury in the

Central Park apartment was a grand piano in the living room. Except for a couch and coffee table, that was about it.

If Diane had little time for decorating, she did make time for friendships. Among her good friends then and now are Joan Ganz Cooney, the brains behind *Sesame Street,* composer Marvin Hamlisch, and columnist Liz Smith.

The Kuralt-Sawyer team broke up in 1982 when Charles left the program. Diane's new coanchor was Bill Kurtis from Chicago. For a time, the ratings remained good. Then they began to dip. There was some talk of friction between Kurtis and Diane.

There was also some criticism of Sawyer herself from detractors. Some characterized her as too "political." They said she was personally responsible for the firings of two executive producers from the show, George Merlis and Bob Ferrante. In a book about CBS, author Peter McCabe said that when Sawyer started to disfavor Ferrante she began to complain about him and Merlis to the CBS news president.

Other Sawyer critics said that she lacked the "nonthreatening quality" that viewers like in the morning when they aren't quite awake. In a *TV Guide* article, a colleague said that Diane was "just too radiant, too brilliant." Perhaps so. But that brilliance would prove just right for *60 Minutes,* one of the top news television shows on the air.

7

Breaking the Barrier

Diane Sawyer found out she was going to be hired for *60 Minutes* in an unusual way. It happened while she was still working on the *Morning* show.

"One day my assistant burst into my office with a bulletin. She had just heard Don [Hewitt, long-time producer of *60 Minutes*] tell a CBS seminar he hoped I would be able to join the *60 Minutes* team. He hadn't mentioned dates, but to me it seemed like the equivalent of reading in the parish notes that the pope wants to name you a cardinal. . . . I was pleased. I was honored. I was afraid it wasn't true."

According to rumor, Hewitt had offered the spot to only one other woman besides Diane. Some three years earlier, the offer, supposedly, went to the well-known newswoman Barbara Walters, who turned down the job. That's the story, although Hewitt denies it.

But the story that Diane heard *was* true. Don Hewitt *was* interested in hiring Sawyer. Hewitt recalls the period when they were discussing her possible move over to *60 Minutes* as the beginning of their mutual admiration society. "Diane was working so hard to impress me that she was the one for *60 Minutes* that she didn't notice I was working just as hard to impress her that *60 Minutes* was the one for her."

For Diane, *60 Minutes* was more than just a job that paid a lot of money. (It did.) It was more than just a job that made her even better known. (It did.) It meant more to her than being the "first woman" to do something. (Although she *was* the first woman to join the show.) It was a challenge for her to be a part of what she considers one of the finest news teams in the business.

So Diane joined *60 Minutes* to become part of the best. Life was different after she left the wee morning hours. Different, but just as hectic. Instead of waking at one or two A.M. to head for the studio, Diane was likely to fly to five different places in a given week, working on several stories. The *60 Minutes* correspondents work on twenty to twenty-five stories a year and log about 200,000 air miles yearly taping those stories. For example, she could fly on Tuesday to Louisiana to interview some military personnel for an upcoming story about the armed forces. On Wednesday she might have gone to Washington, D.C., for research on a story about Pentagon spending. Then she might have flown to Chicago for an in-depth interview with a well-known novelist about a new book.

The original proposal more than twenty years ago for the *60 Minutes* show was: "Why don't we try to package sixty minutes of reality as attractively as Hollywood packages sixty minutes of make-believe?" That's just what Hewitt and his people have successfully achieved, week after week, for two decades.

The program has been called a "fuzzy mix of journalism and showbiz." Indeed, it may be. The interviews have ranged from Henry Kissinger to Johnny Carson, from Corazon Aquino to John McEnroe. This combination of journalism and showbiz has been given the name "confrontational." The correspondents prod and probe, trying to get to the bottom of things. Whether it is Mike Wallace, who is known to be tough, Harry Reasoner, who looks like the man next door, or Morley Safer or Ed Bradley, who are likely to charm the information out of the interviewee, often the result is striking revelation.

Hewitt thought that Diane Sawyer could fit in well with this crew, as was obvious in her *Morning* interview with Nixon. Another time on the *Morning* show during which she showed courage was when she teased England's Prince Charles into telling about some of the antics of his misbehaving younger brother Andrew. Buck-

Diane Sawyer and the rest of the *60 Minutes* crew.

ingham Palace had specifically requested CBS not to ask about Andrew's behavior, but Sawyer did it anyway.

Referring to her own toughness, Diane has said, "Sure, I'm my mother's daughter. I was brought up to be polite to people. But when I'm actually in the middle of an interview and I think someone is being inconsistent or not telling me the truth or thinking they can trick me, then I tend to forget my Emily Post school of journalism. I am up to the suit as much as anyone."

The blustery style that *60 Minutes* fosters is a continuing delight to its audiences, who love to see crooks caught in a lie or celebrities brought down a notch or two. About 20 percent of the stories over the years have been about one kind of swindle or another. Morley Safer has said that "no con man thought he'd made it until he had been on *60 Minutes*."

Along with the confrontation has come public service. Many victims of injustice have been freed as a result of publicity from a *60 Minutes* story. An example was a schoolteacher in New Jersey who was convicted of a kidnapping that in reality never happened. Just the beginning investigation by a *60 Minutes* crew was enough to encourage a new look at the case in the local community. By the time the story aired, the man was out of prison and back in the classroom.

60 Minutes has also given much publicity to many areas of health and medical research. Such diseases as Reye's syndrome (a fatal brain swelling in childhood), Huntington's chorea (a rare, inherited disease that is usually fatal by the fortieth year of life), and Alzheimer's (a disease that brings on senility in elderly people) first became known to large numbers of people after they were given time on segments of *60 Minutes*. People who were unable to walk have been encouraged by seeing shows that demonstrated new electronic aids that help those in wheelchairs or on crutches to become mobile again.

60 Minutes proved to be different from any show before it. In many similar shows, a camera crew was sent out to get the story; the correspondent went along merely to read a few words of explanation for the audience. But on *60 Minutes*, the correspondent is far more important. Although producers are involved, the correspondent has a good deal of interaction with what is being filmed. If the story is a profile of a football player, for instance, the correspondent is as likely to toss a football at the star as he or she is to interview him. If the story is about hot-air ballooning, the viewers watch as the *60 Minutes* correspondent goes "up, up, and away" into the air. The show became a success largely because the audience could see what Hewitt has called "the give and take." He has said, "People are not interested in issues; they are interested in people."

Following that belief, the *60 Minutes* staff is just as interested in dramatic impact and ways to capture an audience as it is in covering something currently in the news. As a result, there is occasional confusion about the show's methods. Don Hewitt has said, "Viewers often think we are giving someone the *60 Minutes* stamp of approval just because we interview him. Viewers who were shocked at our interviewing South Africa's prime minister wrote and said, 'Surely, you wouldn't have interviewed Adolf Hitler in the midst of the Holocaust.' To which I replied, 'Damned right we would.' Despicable as he was, he was the biggest newsmaker of his time."

Actually, the show's title is an exaggeration. The program is about forty-seven minutes long. The three main features per program take about thirteen minutes each. Andy Rooney gets three minutes for his witty commentary, and five minutes are given to introducing the correspondents (the same tape is used for each show), a quick look at each story, letters from the viewers, and end credits. The rest of the time goes to commercials, of course; "bumpers" that plug what's coming up next on the channel; and transitions—the famous ticking clock and the like.

Both producers and correspondents suggest story ideas. Sometimes a big newsmaker will get a call from every one of the *60 Minutes* correspondents on the same day! Each one is trying to get to the source first. That happened in 1988 to Ivan Boesky, the Wall Street tycoon who was later convicted of illegal insider stock trading and went to prison.

Once a story is selected for the program, both the producers and the correspondents make a list of pertinent questions. The two lists are merged, and the story is investigated. The producers start the ball rolling in the field, doing the reporting and editing. That may take six to eight weeks. Sawyer, or any correspondent on the story, could be called in at any time along the way to interview or narrate. However, usually the correspondent spends only eight or ten days on the story when the total time is added up. Why don't the producers themselves present the story on the air since they spend more time with it? The answer is that the correspondents are better broadcasters; that's their job. Diane herself said, "The producer is a reporter. There are two fully equipped reporters on every job. Only one of them has to get hair spray and go on the air."

Once a story is underway, the temporary title is put on a big blackboard in the *60 Minutes* offices. The blackboard has five columns, one for each correspondent. The story's working title is put in the column of the correspondent who is working with it. When the story is all finished, it gets a number. The number is its exact running time, for example, twelve minutes, seventeen seconds, or thirteen minutes, five seconds. For each weekly broadcast, stories are chosen for both their length (so that they balance out to the correct time) and their content (so that each is different from the other). There would never be three interviews with celebrities on one show, for example.

Success brings success, and it also brings imitation. The *60 Minutes* format has been widely imitated since it first began. The show was the first on network news to ask for comments from its audience. Other shows now do it. Imitation doesn't always bring success to the imitator, however. Although ABC has had good results with its *20/20,* NBC hasn't done as well with the news magazine programs it has tried.

Is Diane Sawyer a good interviewer? Apparently so. One CBS news producer said, "She has the skill of a surgeon—she gets under her subject's skin, but without drawing blood."

In what way was Diane different from the other correspondents during an interview? When asked about her interviewing methods, Sawyer says she has a penchant for detail. "I like the way you can see the world in the grains of sand. I'll stop in the middle of the piece and show you what they have for breakfast." Her intuitive thrust with people has sometimes been called a *"divining rod,"* as she seems to get to the heart of each person. Sawyer also talks abut a tendency to overcompensate. "I always read the extra book. I get there earlier than anybody else and I make those extra phone calls." One magazine article compared Diane's reporting methods to the skills of a teacher (which her mother was). The article said, "Is there not, in Diane, something reminiscent of that one grade school teacher that all of us adored? And is there not, in her *60 Minutes* role, something of the civics teacher holding class once a week?"

Most viewers and coworkers liked Diane on *60 Minutes,* but not everyone did. Tom Shales, the television commentator for the *Washington Post,* was once asked how he would fill out Diane Sawyer's "report card" so far. He replied, "Incomplete. I don't think she's really burned up the show. Either she hasn't gotten the great assignments or she hasn't worked hard enough to make them special. If she disappeared from the show, you wouldn't notice."

Some of Diane's interviews were with important political figures. Sometimes they were given a unique view of Diane herself (as when she asked then Vice-President George Bush about the "wimp factor" in his future candidacies). Other times they gave a new look to the person being interviewed. Once she did a profile of

Imelda Marcos, wife of the deposed dictator of the Philippines, and she got Imelda to sing! Another time she interviewed crusty old Admiral Hyman Rickover in his first interview in twenty-eight years (also his last, as it turned out). During their talk, the admiral cheerfully admitted that he had taken gifts from defense contractors, a highly unethical thing to do!

Although Diane is persistent and dedicated in going after a story, she also can be utterly relaxed and friendly with coworkers.

Dean Dominick P. Purpura, Albert Einstein College of Medicine, shows Diane the plaque that honors her achievements.

She talks to building maintenance people as naturally as she talks to the Soviet premier. She has, as they say, "a way with people," and they genuinely like her. Maybe that's why she gets people to reveal themselves during an interview before they are aware of it.

Diane Sawyer was one of six women honored for outstanding accomplishments at the thirty-fourth annual Spirit of Achievement luncheon at the New York chapter of the National Women's Division of the Albert Einstein College of Medicine of Yeshiva University on May 18, 1988. The luncheon benefited AIDS research. Journalists, sculptors, and politicians were honored. Diane Sawyer was chosen for her achievements in television journalism.

8

60 Minutes Segments

Let's take a closer look at what Diane Sawyer, former weathergirl from Louisville, does for a living. Some of her segments on *60 Minutes* are good examples of what she does best. They have included some heart-warming success stories, some that exhibit compassionate human interest, and some that are just funny.

One success story was aired on March 27, 1988. It was entitled "For Their Own Welfare" and told the story of women formerly on welfare who were "making it" in the business world.

Four years before, the Women's Economic Development Corporation, or WEDCO, decided to help prepare women on welfare to run businesses of their own. This St. Paul, Minnesota, organization is a private group funded by Kathy Keeley. She and her associates were bucking the odds. How could they turn around a pattern of living that these welfare women have known for years? How could they break the "welfare cycle"? How could women without much experience in working for others hope to work for themselves?

Kathy Keeley and WEDCO were determined to provide the training. One of their "students" was Tanya Young, a single parent on welfare with a dream for her future. Today Tanya Young has made that dream come true. She designs, makes, and sells a line of children's clothing called Sweet Peas. She is off welfare.

Another success for WEDCO was Ellie Richardson. She has been on and off the welfare rolls for over thirty years. Today she is president and owner of the Salt and Pepper Cleaning Company. Seven people work for her. Said Richardson, "I fired welfare."

WEDCO trained Linda Turney, who used to go to soup kitchens for her meals. Today she runs a day care center. They also trained Laura Mueller, who operates a labeling and mailing service.

How did WEDCO succeed? Kathy Keeley got grants and donations to keep WEDCO afloat and the dreams of these women alive. The corporation trained them in business practices, including how to act with confidence in the business world. The women learned to sell their ideas to banks and other institutions with money so they could secure loans to launch their businesses.

"We're creating role models for other welfare women," said Keeley. WEDCO provides choices, options, and hopes, as well as opportunity.

When Diane Sawyer interviewed Tanya Young for *60 Minutes,* she asked, "What's been the moment you savored the most in all this?" Young replied, "Seeing my clothes in the store and seeing someone buy them. That's really exciting. Big time."

To Ellie Richardson, Sawyer said, "Ellie, I heard you're out there shouting, 'Free at last.' "

"Free at last," the former welfare recipient echoed. "I can pay the bills at last."

"Are you going to make it?" Sawyer asked Tanya Young.

She replied, "Yes. Without a doubt."

One woman who made it was interviewing another who was about to. On that segment Diane Sawyer showed, by her choice of this story for the show, her interest in helping other women "make it big" as well.

Diane at her desk in a rare moment of relaxation.

Another of Sawyer's success stories on *60 Minutes* was of quite a different nature. This compassionate human interest segment had far-reaching consequences after it was aired in January 1985.

Actually, the segment was not particularly newsworthy, although Diane obviously felt it deserved attention. It centered on a young boy in the country of Mali.

The Republic of Mali, in the heart of West Africa, is about the size of California and Texas combined. This landlocked grassy plain has known very hard times, especially since the early 1970s. The people of Mali live mainly by agriculture. They grow rice, peanuts, and cotton, among other crops. However, in 1973–1974, disaster struck the small African nation. There was a famine. Lack of rainfall parched the land so that the farmers could not grow enough crops to feed the people. During the famine period, as many as 100,000 people died.

The people of Mali struggled to overcome the great famine. But disaster struck again, this time in the 1980s, with another drought. Many parts of Africa are still trying to overcome the famine that resulted. Life is still very hard for them. Many people, including many children, have died.

The famine story had taken Diane and her camera crew to a "feeding camp" in Mali, about eight miles from the city of Gao. At the camp, U.S. Army engineers, stationed in Gao for more than six months, were trying to help the famine-stricken people.

Diane recalled that while she was walking about the camp looking for sites to film for *60 Minutes,* she heard a child speaking English. So began her short but far-reaching interview with young Mohammed. He told her that he was either eleven or seventeen years old. He didn't know which. As is true in a number of African lands, his birth had not been recorded.

As Diane remembers, Mohammed was the "skinniest child in the feeding camp." He had learned English from the engineers, who had unofficially adopted him as a sort of mascot. They were trying without much success to "fatten him up."

Diane could not believe how thin and starved the young boy was. "He ate everything." she said, recalling that she and the camera crew took him into Gao for meals. He was so hungry that he reacted like a starved animal. In fact, Mohammed weighed only eighty-four pounds.

Despite the efforts of the *60 Minutes* crew, it seemed clear to Diane, and probably to the viewing audience, that Mohammed could not live very long. He was simply too emaciated, too starved for his body to return to normal. His future looked bleak indeed.

As a horrified American television audience watched, Mohammed told Diane Sawyer how he watched children die of starvation and disease every day. He said he was always hungry himself. At night, his only bed was the ground.

The touching interview between Diane Sawyer and young Mohammed of Mali lasted just forty-five seconds. The impression it created changed Mohammed's life forever.

In August of that year, CBS reran the *60 Minutes* show that contained Diane's interview with Mohammed. Among the viewers this time was Cheryl Carter-Shotts of Indiana. She watched as though in a trance as Diane spoke of the famine in Mali, how children like Mohammed were forced to dig roots and berries from the ground as their only source of food. Long after the rerun had ended, Cheryl could not get the starved boy out of her mind.

When Cheryl's husband returned home that evening, she told him about what she had seen. So began Mohammed's chance at life.

Cheryl and Charlie Shotts had three grown children, but they decided to adopt Mohammed. They would bring him to America and into their home.

But could they? How?

Cheryl called a friend of hers, Reverend Peter Michael, who had just returned from an African trip. His parents had been missionaries and he himself had grown up in Africa, in Nigeria. Michael still had lots of friends and contacts there. Would he help? Cheryl asked. The minister tried, but to no avail.

Cheryl Shotts, however, was a determined woman. Next, she wrote to Diane Sawyer. The letter was followed by a telephone conversation between the two women. Diane was very sympathetic, and they talked for a long time. Yet Diane had to be truthful. She told Cheryl that there was little chance of saving Mohammed, even if they could get him out of the country. He was so malnourished, so close to starving to death.

Cheryl persisted. Missionaries in Mali were contacted. They, too, had little optimism about Mohammed's future. Indeed, the picture was not hopeful. Besides his constant hunger, Mohammed had worms, a clubfoot, a hump on his back, and perhaps tuberculosis as well.

Cheryl and Charlie Shotts were not to be put off. With more than $5,000 of their own savings and a $7,000 loan, Charlie went off to Mali. He was determined to bring back Mohammed. It wasn't easy. The Malinese government demanded all sorts of documents for his release, and the boy's uncles had to be bribed as well. Their price for handing over the young boy was food for one year. Charlie Shotts paid gladly.

It worked! Charlie returned to America with a sickly young boy in his care. No one was more surprised than Diane Sawyer on the day she received another phone call from Indianapolis. It was true; Mohammed was in Indiana. She couldn't believe it. However, she and her camera crew were quickly on the way to film the happy homecoming.

When Diane saw Mohammed, Cheryl Shotts remembers, she "flew to him, buried her face in his neck, and sobbed over and over;" saying, "I thought I'd never see you again."

Diane invited Mohammed to visit her in New York City, and she sent him flowers when his clubfoot was operated on. The Shotts family had only praise for her professionalism. They called her a "beautiful person" and "down to earth." Cheryl was amazed that Diane interviewed them for an entire day without ever taking a single note.

The crew of *60 Minutes* returned again to Indianapolis on the day Mohammed's cast was removed from his repaired foot. In three months' time he had gained thirteen pounds and had grown two inches.

It looked like a happy ending to what began as a sad, forty-five-second interview halfway around the world. And the interview didn't stop there, for it helped other Malinese children to a better life, too. The Shotts family founded Americans for African Adoptions, in hopes of getting other U.S. families interested in taking starving African children into their homes. To Mohammed's great delight, one of the children who came to the United States and was adopted was his best friend from the feeding camp, a boy named Nimit. Better yet, Nimit's new family lived in Bloomington, also in Indiana.

When Diane Sawyer saw Mohammed again, she asked him what he wanted to do after he finished school. He replied, "I want to join *60 Minutes*."

"You mean you want my job?" Diane asked.

"No," he answered. "By that time you'll be doing something else."

As it turned out, young Mohammed Shotts was right.

Of course, not all of Sawyer's segments on *60 Minutes* have had such human interest or been so dramatic or serious. A few of her stories were just plain fun. Take the profile of zany comedian/actor Steve Martin, for instance. Titled "A Wild and Crazy Guy," it was first seen on April 10, 1988.

Diane began the interview by asking Martin to analyze why audiences generally found him so funny. He replied, "I don't really try to make people laugh. I try to think of something that surprises me. . . . You're there to surprise yourself, and ultimately maybe you'll surprise them."

Sawyer let her television audience into Martin's home. This brought back memories of the old *Person to Person* show in the earlier days of television. Famed CBS reporter Edward R. Murrow would bring television audiences into celebrities' living rooms every Friday night for a glimpse at how the famous lived.

Diane told her viewers, "Home to Steve Martin is a stark white modern Beverly Hills house that faces inward on a swimming pool. It has no front windows, and he likes it that way. Off stage, the antic exhibitionist is a kind of introvert who likes to read philosophy."

In the house, Diane got Martin's wife, British actress Victoria Tennant, to talk about her confusion when she first started going out with her future husband. He seemed like a perfectly normal fellow, she said, at first. But people would shout at him in the street, make a lot of noise, and say strange-sounding things. Not being familiar with Martin's career history and his comic routines, she did not understand that people were just reacting to his crazy antics on television. Victoria was very confused. One day she asked him what she was missing. Was it something to do with his past life? "Just what is this wild and crazy guy?" she asked. According to her, Martin replied, "If I tell you, you won't like me anymore."

Sawyer's profile of Steve Martin revealed several sides to the zany man's personality. His private collection of modern art, she says, rivals the best in the country and is certainly a serious interest. Yet the zaniness is never far out of sight. Pointing to a spot that usually held a painting that was at the time being displayed elsewhere, he said, "It's good the picture's out. It's good for it to get out and meet other pictures."

The multitalented Martin also plays a mean banjo. Although he now concentrates on films, he has had a successful stand-up comedy act. Sawyer commented, "It's another Martin trademark that when he masters something, he moves on. He walked away from the stand-up act when he was still drawing crowds of 20,000 people, at the time the largest crowds in the history of live comedy." She asked, "Do you have a gift for not staying so long that you burn out, or staying so long that you become unwelcome?" Martin responded, "I remember saying . . . you can do stand-up too long; they eventually ask you to sit down."

Diane gave her viewers a good look at some of Martin's current interest, the films. Some, like *Pennies from Heaven,* have not been well received, but she didn't shy away from discussing them. Others have been hits, such as *Little Shop of Horrors* and, more recently, *Roxanne,* for which Martin spent two and a half years writing the screenplay himself.

Sawyer connected the premise of *Roxanne* to Martin's actual life. The film is a takeoff on the play *Cyrano de Bergerac,* written by the French playwright Edmond Rostand in 1897. The central character in Rostand's play is an intellectual who is skilled at dueling and has an inordinately long nose. Cyrano, like Steve Martin, had hidden talents that most people were unable to see under the clown's exterior. In Cyrano's case, his hidden talent was the writing of beautiful poetry; for the updated version, wild and crazy guy Steve Martin wrote the love speeches and letters to Roxanne, the title character.

From the fun of Steve Martin to the warmth of Mohammed's story to the hope of new dreams for former welfare women in Minnesota, Diane Sawyer's stories for *60 Minutes* carried the mark of the caring professional.

9

Glamour: the Business and Personal Sides

Diane Sawyer joined *60 Minutes* in 1984. Two years later her contract with CBS was due to be renewed. It caused quite a stir around the network.

At the time CBS and the broadcasting industry as a whole were going through a "slimming-down" period. They were trying to cut costs and save money. Indeed, the CBS network laid off more than one thousand employees in 1986.

Where did this austerity program leave Diane, the newest of the *60 Minutes* correspondents? No one suggested that her job was threatened, but what about her contract?

Those questions were fully answered when Diane Sawyer and CBS signed a new contract. For five years. For, reportedly, $1.2 million per year! Diane was definitely a rising star.

The network industry, like many other industries that involve prominent, well-known personalities, is usually buzzing with rumors. And there certainly were rumors a-plenty before the Sawyer contract was signed. The rumors were usually accompanied by stories in the national newspaper gossip columns. Diane Sawyer is going to NBC, shouted one story. No, to ABC, said another. All three networks are fighting over her, declared still another source. This went on all through the many weeks of negotiations between Diane and CBS before the contract was signed.

The most persistent rumor claimed that what Diane Sawyer really wanted was not a new contract with *60 Minutes*. What she wanted most of all was to be an anchorperson. Most television news viewers, and probably the majority of those in the industry, would name "anchorperson" as the most prestigious spot in the world of broadcast news. The anchorperson is that face you see and recognize night after night on the evening news broadcast, reporting the day's events to you live. The anchorperson is the top spot in the news program, a professional, of course, but also a celebrity, a star.

No one doubted that Diane, if the rumors were true, was qualified to fill the top spot. However, in 1986 the three top spots were already filled—by qualified, competent, well-liked, and very professional people. Tom Brokaw held down the anchor spot at NBC. Peter Jennings anchored ABC. And it was Dan Rather, who had taken over for the noted Walter Cronkite, at CBS. Unless one of these men left the position for some reason, where was there room for Diane?

Rumors persisted. What about a "coanchor" deal, having two people share the top spot on an equal basis? Diane, of course, had shared the spotlight on the *Morning* show with Kuralt. But apparently she did not push for such an arrangement during contract talks. In addition, Dan Rather's contract supposedly gave him veto power over any possible coanchor. He did not ask for Diane to sit beside him.

Although all this was only rumor in 1986, Diane did later admit that the anchor position was the job she wanted. "Women are an important economic and cultural force in this country," she has said. "I think all women look forward to the day when there's a woman as coanchor of the evening news."

In 1986, the top spot, shared or not, did not come to pass. Diane did sign again with CBS. Why? At a salary of more than one million yearly, certainly money was a factor. So was loyalty. Remember Diane and the Nixon years? She felt somewhat the same about CBS; the network had been good to her.

The rumor mill in the network industry often applies certain adjectives to people. A word often applied to Diane is *ambitious*. Is she? What does she think about being called ambitious?

Sometimes the word *ambitious* has been used in a negative way when applied to "career" women. As though it isn't quite "right" for a woman to be concerned about getting ahead in her job. When it's used that way, the word annoys Diane. But if the word is used in the sense of wanting to master one's job, wanting to be the best possible, then Diane would surely agree when people used that word to describe her. She does want to be the best there is at what she does. She is also willing to work long and hard to get there.

Even before Diane Sawyer made another career move in 1989 to that coveted coanchor position, most people would have said that she had it all. She was at the top level in her profession. She was doing work she loved. She had wealth and respect, admiration, and perhaps even envy. Who could ask for more?

Some people might say that the one thing Diane Sawyer has lacked is time. Her own personal time. With such a heavy demanding schedule, what kind of personal life can she have?

Apparently quite a good one. For, not surprisingly, busy Diane Sawyer finds time for other things besides work.

For one, she likes sports and claims to have tried just about every one. But sooner or later, the schedule interferes or her interests change and she gives them up. She used to run and swim, for example, but doesn't do much of either anymore. She does ski and ride horseback when she can, and she frequently plays tennis with NBC anchor Tom Brokaw and his wife.

She still loves to cook and has become quite good. Yet she must also be conscious of putting on weight before the television cameras. At five feet nine inches tall, Diane looks trim at 135 pounds, and she exercises with a rowing machine and sometimes with weights to stay that way. Fortunately, the fact that she doesn't much care for sweets helps to keep a trim body.

If Diane looks trim and glamorous in front of the cameras, her "at-home" outfits are a big contrast. She is apt to be found in jeans and oversize sweaters. According to Diane, the sophisticated suits she wears on television are not her natural style. Actually, she

Diane, Ed Bradley, and CBS anchorman Dan Rather on a *60 Minutes* assignment in Red Square, Moscow.

claims to have very little fashion sense and says that, like musical talent, you're either born with it or you're not. However, she must have some sense of fashion because she chose her own wardrobe for *60 Minutes,* and her choices seemed just right for her.

Much has been made of Diane Sawyer's looks. In a *TV Guide* article, a well-known photographer of beautiful people, Francesco Scavullo, chose Diane as one of the six most beautiful women on television. He said, "Diane Sawyer is a great beauty and a marvelous newscaster with an incredibly personal style."

The slick *Bazaar* magazine has hailed Diane's beauty in one of its features, and Blistex said she had the most beautiful lips on television! (Blistex, which comes in a lipstick-type tube, promotes healing of chapped lips.)

Hardly a month goes by without an article about Diane Sawyer in one of the national magazines. Some praise her work. Some praise her beauty. Some do both. Yet mostly Diane complains about what she reads. Just as she downgraded her looks and accomplishments in high school and college, so she does now. The magazine prints a glamorous picture of her; Diane sees only a pug nose. An article says her hair is beautiful; to Diane it's "baby fine and lousy." And so it goes.

What can one make of a person who is highly acclaimed and yet speaks so negatively of herself? Michael Shnayerson, a magazine writer, has an idea about why she puts herself down so much. He thinks that "beautiful girls sometimes resort to [charming exaggeration] because they sense jealousy in their girl friends, or because the world's adulation seems to be puzzlingly unearned." He thinks that Diane's ambition may stem from the "desire to prove herself worthy of the praise so carelessly heaped upon her for having good looks."

Magazine articles about herself can't possibly take up too much of Diane's reading time, however. She still tries to read at least five newspapers daily and subscribes to more than twenty-five magazines, many of them science-oriented. And serious reading remains a strong interest. Among her favorite authors are Emily Dickinson, Henry James, and George Eliot.

Learning is also high on Sawyer's "off-time" list. For some years she and multimillionaire Mort Zuckerman have been paying a Columbia University (in New York City) professor to give a philosophy course to just the two of them. This study of the history of ideas began with creation, moving up through biblical times and into Greek civilization.

Diane is still a movie fan. She goes on marathon film binges whenever she can, although instead of going to the theater, she may stay up nearly all night at home in front of her VCR. And she admits to sometimes relaxing in the house by dancing to MTV!

Diane Sawyer sounds like a fun person to have as a friend. Once she and Liz Smith (who reports on news and gossip about celebrities on NBC) planned a surprise party for composer Marvin Hamlisch (who wrote the music for the movie *Sting,* among many other credits). They got well-known personalities to fill in the sentence "If I could spend an hour with Marvin Hamlisch . . ." They arranged the responses from such people as Frank Sinatra and Liza Minnelli in a framed collage to present to the delighted Hamlisch. At another party Diane suggested to the guests that everyone reveal "something about yourself you've never told anyone before." That idea didn't get too many takers, however. Her favorite parties of all are songfests. Some guests who have heard her sing say that she has an excellent voice, and "when she sings 'In the Still of the Night,' you're held spellbound."

But even parties or reading or sports can't be everything. What about romance in her life? Back in college at Wellesley, she dated the same Mort Zuckerman who now shares the philosophy course with her. In San Clemente, she was linked with Frank Gannon, her coworker. Then her name began to be seriously linked with Richard Holbrook, former assistant secretary of state and, more recently, managing director of Shearson Lehman Hutton, a well-known investment firm.

A number of Diane's friends thought she and Holbrook were "serious." Dark, handsome Holbrook and Diane spent a good deal of time together in spite of their heavy schedules. He was director of the Peace Corps in Morocco between 1970 and 1972, then returned to Washington to serve in the Carter administration. Friends Tom and Meredith Brokaw thought they would eventually marry. Another friend said, "Diane is comfortable with Dick; if she were the marrying type she'd marry Dick."

"Marrying type" or not, Diane says she always assumed that she would marry one day. "I'm just a late bloomer," she said in one article. In another she said, "I'll probably wake up one morning and say, "This is the day. This is the day to get married."

And that's almost what happened.

Those who thought Diane would eventually marry were right. But those who thought she would eventually marry Richard Holbook were wrong.

During the 1987–1988 television season, after Diane returned from an assignment in Kuwait, the rumor mill started again. It said that Holbrook and Sawyer were no longer seeing each other. Columnists began to report seeing Diane with someone else, the well-known producer-director Mike Nichols. Here and there photographs began to appear in magazines showing them at dinner together.

Like Diane, Nichols has a long list of skills and accomplishments. Born in Berlin on November 6, 1931, he first became famous as part of the comedy team of Elaine May and Mike Nichols. They appeared at New York nightclubs such as the Blue Angel and the Village Vanguard. Their routines mocking social customs propelled them into a popular Broadway show in 1960 called *An Evening with Elaine May and Mike Nichols.*

Eventually Nichols moved behind the scenes, into directing and

Mike Nichols, winner of the "Best Director" Tony award for *The Real Thing*.

producing films and theater shows. He directed Dustin Hoffman in *The Graduate* and Cher in *Silkwood*, and he was involved in such films as *Day of the Dolphins, The Odd Couple, Wall Street,* and many more. On stage his best-known production is probably the musical hit, *Annie*. The work of Nichols has been widely acclaimed. He has won the Antoinette Perry Award (commonly called the Tony) for his stage work, and the New York Film Critics Award for directing movies.

To say that many people were surprised when, after so many years with Richard Holbrook, she began seeing Mike Nichols is an understatement. But they were really shocked on April 29, 1988, when she and Nichols were married in Edgartown, Massachusetts.

Perhaps, as she said earlier, she just woke up and said, "This is the day."

After the wedding ceremony, a reception was held for twelve people in the home of singer Carly Simon and her husband. Then the newlyweds flew back to New York, and later to Europe for a honeymoon.

When Diane Sawyer decides to make changes in her life, she certainly does so in a big way. In 1988 a marriage; and in 1989 a new job!

Early in 1989, rumors flew that Diane Sawyer would be leaving *60 Minutes* and CBS. Those rumors proved to be true. ABC succeeded in wooing Diane away with a sweet contract. On August 3, 1989 ABC launched *Prime Time Live*, with coanchors Diane Sawyer and Sam Donaldson. Sam Donaldson, an established newsman, covered the White House beat during the Reagan years and appeared on *This Week With David Brinkley*. Diane and Sam, in a live prime time news hour, deliver investigative reports on such topics as boarding houses for the aged and the hostage crisis in Beirut. They converse with a studio audience and conduct interviews with such famous folk as Secretary of State James Baker, TV Star Roseanne Barr, and Vice President Dan Quayle. All eyes will be on Diane Sawyer's latest TV venture. Will she remain in her current position? Will she go on to other vistas? Time will tell. After a major career change and a marriage in the space of a year, one thing is for sure, Diane Sawyer is full of surprises.

From her days as Junior Miss, to the frustration of being a "weathergirl," to the never-to-be-forgotten Nixon years, Diane Sawyer has been heading for the top. "Well done," say her friends and coworkers; "we'll be there watching," says her television audience.

For those who haven't yet seen Diane Sawyer at work, a treat is in store. Skilled, competent, knowledgeable, the ultimate professional—she is one of the best in the business. Turn on your television set; she is worth watching.

CHRONOLOGY

1945 — Lila Diane Sawyer is born on December 22.

1963 — Diane wins the Junior Miss Contest.

1967 — Diane graduates from Wellesley College with a Bachelor of Arts degree in English.

— Diane works as a reporter at WLKY in Louisville.

1969 — Diane's father is killed in a tragic automobile accident.

1970 — Diane moves to Washington, D.C. and is hired as an assistant to the White House deputy press secretary.

1972 — The Watergate scandal begins.

1974 — President Richard M. Nixon resigns. Diane and others travel with him to San Clemente, California to organize his papers.

1978 — Diane returns to Washington, D.C. and gets a job at the Washington Bureau of CBS News as a general assignment reporter.

1979 — Diane covers the Three Mile Island nuclear reactor crisis.

1981 — Diane begins coanchoring the morning news show on CBS, retitled *Morning With Charles Kuralt and Diane Sawyer*.

1982 — Diane interviews former President Nixon for her morning news program.

— Charles Kuralt leaves the morning show. Bill Kurtis becomes Diane's new coanchor.

1984 — Diane becomes the first female correspondent on *60 Minutes*.

1986 — Diane renews her CBS contract.

1988 — Diane marries producer-director Mike Nichols on April 29.

   — Diane is honored at the thirty-fourth annual Spirit of Achievent luncheon on May 18.

1989 — Diane signs a contract with ABC to coanchor the *Prime Time Live* news program.

INDEX

Gill Memorial Library
Broad and Commerce
Paulsboro, NJ 08066
(609) 423-5155